"A message worth con.
Publishers Week.,

"A blowtorch to the bars of a cage."
Bookpage.com

"Whoa! Batten down the hatches, and leave what you think
you already know at the door."
Carry Graham

"Gritty. Deep. A message to rattle your cage, and change the world."
Lucas Farrell

"Like a tuning fork to what lay sleeping within our own hearts."
Ken Dahl, Author of *What is God, And How Does It Work?*

"Inner Anarchy is not a book; it's smelling salts."
Jacob Byrne

"This book has changed everything I thought I knew about God."
Byron Johnson

"A sign post in the middle of the desert pointing
the way to inner truth."
Donna Willis Kinnaird

"An admonition to the Christian church,
an invitation to birth a new world, and a challenge
to tear down what is ruling us from within."
Maria Armstrong

INNER ANARCHY

DETHRONING GOD AND JESUS
TO SAVE OURSELVES AND THE WORLD

JIM PALMER

Divine Nobody Press

Inner Anarchy
Dethroning God and Jesus to Save Ourselves and the World

Published in 2014 by Divine Nobody Press.
Printed in 2014.

All scripture quotations, unless otherwise indicated, are taken from the WORLD ENGLISH BIBLE®. Used by permission of Rainbow Missions, Inc., http://WorldEnglishBible.org.

The author apologizes for any errors or omissions and would be grateful if notified of any corrections that should be incorporated in future reprints or editions of this book.

ISBN-13: 978-1503174481
ISBN-10: 1503174484

Also by Jim Palmer

Divine Nobodies:
Shedding Religion to Find God
(and the unlikely people who help you)

Wide Open Spaces:
Beyond Paint-by-Number Christianity

Being Jesus in Nashville:
Finding the Courage to Live Your Life
(Whoever and Wherever You Are)

Notes from (Over) the Edge:
Unmasking the Truth to End Your Suffering

Dedicated to all the dreamers who dare to imagine and birth a new world.

ACKNOWLEDGMENTS

THIS BOOK WOULD NOT HAVE BEEN POSSIBLE WITHOUT THE HELP AND SUPPORT OF MANY AMAZING PEOPLE.

As mentioned previously, throughout the process I sent draft chapters to a reader group that offered invaluable input. Their feedback wasn't always easy to hear, but it scares me to think of what this book would have been without their involvement, which, for starters, would have probably been 20,000 words longer! I owe a great debt of gratitude to each of them and their contribution to how this book ultimately shaped up.

This book was an independent publishing effort, and several people offered their time and skills to make it happen. Friend and professional photographer, Darla Winn, did an original photo for the cover. Yana Cortlund designed the cover and interior pages of the book for publication. I've had the good fortune of having Darla and Yana contribute their time, gifts, and skills to my work as an author. Not only are they a couple of my favorite people, but they are extraordinarily talented in what they do. Becca Tyndall Cipriani and Diana Blair Revell edited and copyedited the manuscript, for which I am deeply grateful. I have written five books, but don't assume I'm an expert in syntax and grammar. If you don't believe me, just ask Becca and Diana! The readability and flow of this book has a lot to do with the work they did.

In every book I have written, there always seems to be an unexpected person who pops up and plays a significant role in the process. In this book, it was Brian Sage. Several years ago, Brian and I bumped into each other in an online forum. Brian's comments resonated with me and we struck up a friendship. He has always encouraged me to turn to that higher spiritual presence within me. Brian has spent much of his life connecting people to that source in a unique way. A former sheep-and-cattle farmer, Brian lives in New Zealand. He and his wife, Robin, founded River Valley, an outdoor adventure lodge situated beside the Rangitikei River in the Taihape hill country, New Zealand. Now owned by daughter Nicola and her husband, Brian, and managed by granddaughter Janey, the lodge draws people from all over the world to take part in river rafting and horse trekking or just to relax and enjoy a beautiful environment. It has become a place that helps people make a natural connection to their deep feelings and what is real inside them. I am most grateful for Brian sharing his life experiences and insights along the way in the writing of this book.

Writing a book is a major endeavor, which involves a tremendous commitment of time and energy. I could not have pulled this off without the unwavering encouragement, support, and patience of Heather. She was always the first to read the chapters, and she cleaned up the manuscript considerably before it was sent off to the copyedit stage. Heather is a spiritual but not religious person, and so her feedback and input were very important. If it passed the Heather Test, I knew I was on the right track!

A lot happened in my life over the course of writing this book. Jessica started driving, Cera entered middle school, and Whitney went to Japan with the Navy. Oh yeah, and we adopted a greyhound—Gin! Most Sunday mornings, Jessica and I go to a local coffee shop to drink coffee and chat. Those little conversations always leave a big impression on my heart, and in many ways impacted the writing of this book. I'm really hoping we can get this no-death thing out of the way soon. I wouldn't mind having another several thousand years of those Sunday mornings.

So many friends I have made and connected with through Facebook and social media have been instrumental in my journey from the beginning and certainly in the writing and publishing of *Inner Anarchy*. They have graciously and enduringly offered their encouragement, support, and input and contributed the financial resources to make this book happen. Jesus said, "Without me you can do nothing." Well, I'm also quite sure that I wouldn't have made it very far without all these folks who have stood with me along the way.

INTRODUCTION

JESUS.

Perhaps no person in history has been the subject of so much controversy and debate. It began two thousand years ago, when religious and political powers conspired to brutally execute him. Virtually all modern scholars of antiquity agree that Jesus existed historically. After that point, agreement is difficult to find; opinions about the life and message of Jesus differ sharply. The Jew of Jesus' day saw him as demonic and dangerous—a false messiah, heretic, and the worst of blasphemers. In Islam, Jesus is seen as a messenger of God who performed miracles. Humanists and others who claim no religious faith emphasize the humanity and social teachings of Jesus. And then there is Christianity. Christians claim Jesus as their own and consider themselves the ones who truly speak for him.

Where is Jesus?

Is he dead and gone? Is he alive? If so, where is he? In heaven? And what and where is heaven exactly? Is he coming back?

How? When? Why?

The Christian religion teaches that Jesus died to atone for the sins of the world, rose from the dead, and will return one future day to perform God's final judgment. But twenty centuries later, there is still no Jesus.

Why the delay? Where is he?

The world has assumed that the Christian religion represents the life, message, and teachings of Jesus. But that view is changing. People are fed up and leaving the church, repulsed by its hypocrisy, irrelevance to the suffering in the world, greed, and fear-based doctrines of a wrathful God who saves a few chosen ones and sends the rest to eternal hell. In their heart of hearts, people are recognizing that many of the traditional teachings of the Christian religion are shams. The spirit of the times is shifting. People are no longer accepting the answers and explanations they have been given. They are becoming more confident in thinking for themselves and listening to their inner voice of truth.

The time is ripe for the dawning of a new age, but it will require rebellion. We cannot move forward without anarchy—inner anarchy. We must be liberated from the dominion of religion. We must dethrone and tear down the mindsets and ideologies that are ruling our world from within us and taking us further down a road of certain doom. Once we displace the old ruling system within us, we set the stage for the salvation of our world to unfold.

But there's some work yet to do in the Christian religion. For the past two thousand years, rather than preparing the world for the return of the messiah, Christianity has been standing in the way of the birth of a new age. This is the day of reckoning. The established doctrines and mindsets of men are blocking the way for our world to be saved. They must be dismantled and torn down one by one. They have hidden and obscured the true message of Jesus long enough.

The guardians, preachers, and teachers of the Christian religion must now set things right and give the real messiah back to the world!

Jesus announced the inauguration of a new age—the likes of which we have never seen but have dreamed of. His words are compelling and fascinating. He implied that this age is hidden in the human heart and is now ready to be birthed into existence. Jesus said it would come in the midst of great turmoil and would be led not by religious preachers and Bible scholars, but by those who open up their minds, become like a child and trust what is deep inside their hearts.

Are you willing to become that little child and trust what you feel deep inside you?

"And he said: 'Truly I tell you, unless you change and become elemental and trusting like little children, you will never enter the kingdom of heaven'" (Matt. 18:3).

CHAPTER ONE

*The old order of this world is beginning
to break down, and it's very distressing.*

OUR WORLD IS BROKEN.

I'm sure this is not news to anyone.

The planet is in crisis—the planet itself and the human race inhabiting it. We face the possible destruction of the planet's delicate ecosystems as well as the proliferation of weapons of mass destruction. With rising rates of poverty, homelessness, crime, mental illness, substance abuse, social isolation, apathy, and dehumanization, the current human situation is dominated by horror, suffering, and pain. So many of us are masking lives of loneliness, emptiness, anxiety, unhappiness, and despair.

Have we gone crazy? What is wrong with us? What are we doing to ourselves?

News headlines are filled with yet another tragedy, humanitarian crisis, or natural disaster. We look for a scapegoat, feeling helpless and frustrated with little hope on the horizon. Most of us try to do the best we can, but we know something is desperately wrong.

How many of us live behind a brave front that covers the disappointments of so many lost dreams? In our pursuit of peace, security, happiness, and well-being, we work so hard, but the payoff is so small. We have mixed and matched together several life scenarios in an attempt to be happy, but the happiness doesn't last. And if you're like me, you've experienced more than your fair share of disappointment and heartache

1

in the process: tragedy, sickness, financial stress and struggle, loss of loved ones, rejection from partners, and suffering by our children. This world can be so unforgiving. We do not dwell on these things, but they take their toll. Depression in our society is epidemic.

With all our intelligence and ingenuity, we were supposed to have a simpler, better, more relaxed, loving modern life, but it's becoming more tense and complex each day.

The wealthy elite claim we're evolving into a better humanity. And maybe their status and means occasionally let them live in that reality. Maybe. But for the average person, true democracy and equality seem to be just a dream. The spiritual gurus speak of a "higher reality" and say that we can attract to ourselves anything we want if we want it bad enough. Tell that to our teens who are confused and struggling, cutting and killing themselves, imprisoned by lies about what it means to be worthy and significant. Each day another religious, business, or political leader or sports hero is exposed as a liar, cheater, abuser, criminal, or fraud.

The insanity of our world has become the new normal that we live by day and watch by night on TV reality shows. What is happening to us? Our whole world is heading into an out-of-control, aggressive, emotional drama. Are we all going mad?

We have every technological advantage, made countless medical advancements, accumulated vast knowledge about ourselves and our universe, and have endless options to amuse, entertain, and improve ourselves. And yet we are facing extinction-level problems.

Why are things not getting better? We are so smart. Shouldn't we have figured this out by now? Haven't we tried everything?

We have put our faith in government, religion, philosophy, psychology, philanthropy, science, technology, and economics, but a quick scan of the daily news shows that none of those are working. Is trying harder really the answer? Some of our planet's best-intentioned, most brilliant, passionate, dedicated people have poured themselves into every field imaginable. If those avenues could have solved our dilemma, they would have by now.

Aren't we tired yet? Haven't we suffered long enough?

Civilizations have come and gone. Empires have risen and fallen. Great eras of human history have rolled in and receded like the tide. And the wheels on the bus go round and round.

What about God?

I never gave a second thought to whether God existed. I was taught that there was an all-knowing and all-powerful God up above, directing the course of human history and worldly affairs. My life was predicated upon the idea that we could change our world and make things better with the help of God. That was my conviction. I sincerely wanted to make a difference. I cared. I had faith that this would happen. How could it not? With God, all things are possible!

But where is this all-powerful God? And why does human misery and suffering persist? It doesn't line up. If I were truly "all-powerful," I am quite sure I'd have straightened out the mess of our world by now.

The explanations that religious leaders offer about this dilemma don't make sense:

> *"We don't understand, but it's all a part of his great plan."*
>
> *"God works in mysterious ways."*
>
> *"We just have to trust God."*
>
> *"His ways are not our ways."*

In a nutshell, this religious narrative supports the following assumptions:

1. God created a world in which suffering and misery are inevitable.

2. Though an all-powerful God is capable of intervening and changing this scenario, it's part of his mysterious divine plan not to do so.

3. Instead, God has supplied everything we need to work this out, but we can't get it right.

4. This is all our fault, so one day in the future, God will swoop down and set everything straight.

Seriously?

The old order of this world is beginning to break down, and it's very distressing. The people who made the promises, societal institutions, and structures that were to solve our problems and make things work and the ideas and knowledge that were supposed to carry us forward into a grand future have not delivered. Many people are now seeing that our God explanations don't make logical sense. There is no shining light on the horizon that we can look toward with real hope. No . . . not anywhere.

The definition of "doomed" is "likely to have an unfortunate and inescapable outcome." Yep, that about sums it up! Or, as the Urban Dictionary puts it, "to be irreversibly and completely fucked."

CHAPTER TWO

We have been led to believe that our world is being guided along by some kind of divine or scientific evolutionary plan.

BELIEVE ME. I MOST DEFINITELY GAVE THE GOD-AND-RELIGION ROUTE A GO OF IT.

I went to seminary, earned a master of divinity degree, and became an ordained minister. I served as the senior pastor of a successful Christian church. But despite my noble intentions, good theology, and dedication, the world didn't change. Neither did our city, our congregation, or even myself. We did a lot of good and some lasting relationships were born out of people's involvement. But despite all the biblical teaching, worship gatherings, small groups, and outreach programs of our ministry, anxiety, loneliness, emptiness, dysfunction, turmoil, and unhappiness persisted in people's lives. It was not noticeable in church on Sunday mornings or Wednesday nights, but I saw it behind the scenes through my involvement in people's daily lives. It was true of my own life. Something was desperately amiss, and I grew increasingly disillusioned. After twenty-something years of Christian ministry, I resigned my position.

Leaving professional ministry and organized church behind, I set out to determine what—if anything—of my Christian faith was real. I began writing books about my journey of shedding religion to find God.

The first two books I wrote (*Divine Nobodies* and *Wide Open Spaces*) share the part of my journey in which I began questioning and scrutinizing all my Christian beliefs. Actually, I didn't question all of them at first, because I had a few deeply held beliefs that I never considered questioning. But the more I deconstructed my belief system, the less connection I felt with the Christianity I had learned in seminary and preached at church. The overwhelming response to my first two books surprised me. I received countless emails from others who had become disenchanted with and, in many cases, greatly damaged by organized Christianity and had left it behind.

But even as I was becoming more unchristian, my interest in Jesus was growing. It occurred to me that maybe I should be seeking to understand Jesus outside the religious mindset, specifically the Christian religion. I decided to devote a year of my life to search for a deeper, more practical meaning of Jesus, and the story of what happened that year was my third book, *Being Jesus in Nashville.* The book was rejected by my Christian publisher, and my writing contract was swiftly canceled due to said writer's heresy. Perhaps this was a clue that I was on the right track.

After the controversy of *Being Jesus in Nashville*, I decided to write a fourth book, *Notes from (Over) the Edge*, in which I explored the primary ways we are led astray by the mindset and mentalities of religion and how those mentalities have tainted people's understanding of Jesus. Increasingly, I was discovering that Jesus was not a fan of religion and was very outspoken against it. He was appalled by it as much as I was! *Notes* was a book about unlearning the ways we were taught to approach truth and was a challenge to consider an entirely different set of premises about ourselves and what is real. One of the fundamental ideas of religion is that truth and life are found outside ourselves and imparted to us from external sources such as "God," a "higher power," the Bible or other sacred writings, or religious gurus.

But the more I observed Jesus outside of the mindset of religion, the more I picked up on little but powerful insights. For example, Jesus implied that truth and life are somehow found inside ourselves. He even once made the point that we would not find them in the scriptures!

On another occasion, Jesus instructed people to find their heaven inside them. In John 5:39, Jesus reprimanded the religious scholars, saying, "You search the scriptures because you think they give you eternal life. But the scriptures point to me!" And in Luke 17:21, when his disciples asked him about when the kingdom of God would come, Jesus said it was already here.

The more I poured over the life and teachings of Jesus, the more I realized that Jesus was never promoting the idea of some all-powerful God up above, overseeing human history and worldly affairs. Neither did he teach that the current suffering and disharmony of our world is part of some mysterious divine plan that works out in the end. Contrary to popular Christian teaching, Jesus is not going to one day appear in the clouds to rapture people from their earthly misery to a blissful heavenly home. He actually preached quite a different God persona than we have been taught about. His Father was a totally different character!

The Christian church has preached a powerless gospel that has led countless people into a religious maze that goes nowhere. They have handcuffed the masses to a false God. The Bible has been misinterpreted and misused by religious leaders who claim to have spiritual authority, giving this bankrupt system a false air of legitimacy and credibility. I'm not pointing the finger; I was one of them. I was sincere, but I was sincerely wrong.

The only explanation for why an all-powerful God has not been able to help this world is that there isn't one. The reality is that there is no hidden, benevolent intelligence up in the sky or embedded within this physical universe to help us along and rescue us. If there were, we would have identified that God centuries ago, it would be common knowledge to everyone, and this world would be a much different place.

We have been led to believe that our world is being guided along by some kind of divine or scientific evolutionary plan. But if we could empty our minds of all the beliefs, values, narratives, philosophies, and ideologies that we have developed over the centuries to give our life meaning, we would discover that we live in a world with no plan. No matter how much we hype ourselves up, the uncomfortable truth is that there is no built-in blueprint guiding us along. We live by our own resources, and our universe grinds along randomly in obedience to the fixed laws of nature. Science has explained and described these laws, and there is nothing mysterious about them. We live in a space-time existence that somehow had a beginning but will also eventually end—probably in the same chaos in which it began. Our only way out of this is through the grave, and life beyond that is purely speculative.

We have worked hard to make the religious mindset attractive, and we built it using the best we had—the best buildings, the best programs, and the best budgets. Within this religious mindset and system, we have followed the prescribed beliefs and practices for relating to God. And yet our world continues spiraling out of control. In fact, some of the most horrendous atrocities ever inflicted upon humankind occurred in the name of God and religion.

We take our chances with the cards of circumstances randomly dealt to us. Sometimes we win and sometimes we lose. There are no guarantees. We can be here today and gone tomorrow—a precarious position for everyone. Sure, we have done our best to help our situation by designing our customs, rules, and systems. We have even created our own deities, but these are founded on legends and dubious mythologies from the mists of time and primitive thinking. They have never been proven. In the meantime, we do our best to have fun and live our daily lives. We human beings are a smart lot of people, but we have never been able to establish worldwide peace and well-being on our planet.

Have we been missing something?

CHAPTER THREE

If you want to get angry about something, get angry at the false myths and ideologies that are governing our existence.

LOOKING BACK, I REGRET THAT I DID NOT PERFORM MY DUE DILIGENCE SOONER AND EXERCISE MY OWN INDEPENDENT INVESTIGATION.

I blindly accepted and believed what the system taught me about God, Jesus, myself, the Bible, people, the world, and life. For a string of years, I tried my best to somehow make Jesus fit with Christianity, wanting to satisfy the Christian folk who had read my books. But, ultimately, I had to let go of the religious mindset with both hands.

Our world is not working; it is coming apart at the seams. It's human nature to find someone to blame. Republicans blame Democrats, Democrats blame Republicans; Christians blame atheists, atheists blame Christians; Israelis blame Palestinians, Palestinians blame Israelis, etc. My inbox is filled with emails from people expressing their anger toward institutional church and its leaders. We are continuously looking for a scapegoat—it's Obama's fault, it's Mark Driscoll's fault, it's Justin Bieber's fault, it's fill-in-the-blank's fault.

But consider the possibility that the current futility of the world is actually no one's fault. The world is simply the way it is as scientists describe it. There are no people to blame or scapegoat for the suffering and misery of our existence. There is no person or people who are the enemy. Then what is? Isn't the enemy the beliefs that rule and drive us from within, and many of those beliefs have existed for thousands of years?

Solving the crisis of our world is not a matter of removing certain individuals or groups from positions of power. It goes deeper than that. The enemy is not the people, but the attitudes, narratives, mindsets, and belief systems that have poisoned us all and rule in our minds. These are the principalities and powers that have cast a darkness over our world, and they must be challenged and struck down. If you want to get angry about something, get angry at the false myths and ideologies that are governing our existence. Here's something else to get angry about—these ideas, myths, and ideologies are living inside your mind and ruling your life right now!

The way our minds have been trained to reason is fundamentally warped. No matter what avenue (including and especially religion) we search for truth and answers, we are not going to find them. We have been programmed with a kind of reasoning that keeps us locked in a futile world that we cannot escape except through death.

Why is our planet and humankind facing the very real threat of destruction?

It is because we are operating with sets of fixed ideas that have spread like a virus to every aspect of human society, sabotaging any possibility for a surviving, thriving world. It makes no difference where you turn. Religion is no different from politics, which is no different from science, which is no different from our education system, which is no different from pop culture, which is no different from . . . you name it! They have all been infected by the same false premises, and we have been indoctrinated by them. The enemy is not someone or something out there, but is inside each of us in the form of these beliefs.

We are never going to get out of this mess until we confront the reality that our existence (as it is currently unfolding according to these bogus ideas) is futile, doomed, and meaningless. Those religious and worldly beliefs have had their chance. The clock has run out, and it is now time for them to go. We can no longer allow them to rule over us and in us. The current brokenness of our world is the critique against this old order. The conclusion? It is finished! Over! Done!

We need anarchy! It's time to revolt.

Yes, anarchy! Not political anarchy, but inner anarchy, in which we topple, dethrone, defrock, kick out, and cast aside the current ruling ideas that are programmed inside us. Those ideas have failed miserably. They were given plenty of time and opportunity to prove their legitimacy, and they have not succeeded. They cunningly and ruthlessly rule over us and continue to argue and fight among each other on the battleground inside us. This is the day of reckoning. Let all ideologies be put on notice. This is an indictment against all the bankrupt and powerless precepts that are governing our lives from within. They keep driving us relentlessly. Their authority must be decisively stripped away. They block us from being who we truly are. It is time to free ourselves from their power and control. It is anarchy or die!

Those ruling mental constructs must be expelled from within us. They are standing in our way. But they are not going to go easily. As futile as they are, they have become our security and our friends, and we fear striking out from them in independence. We have all built our little kingdoms and worldly statuses by using these beliefs, so they accuse the hell out of us if we try to drop them. We must get unreasonable to overthrow the current system that is ruling our world from inside our psyches. The old system is not going to fade quietly into the night without a fight. Our habitual way of reasoning has a titanic amount of energy driving our world and lives forward. We must unplug ourselves from the source of these powerless ideas.

We have to wake up! It is time to overthrow the system of ideas that rules our world and fills our heads.

Instead, what we have done so far is replace old ideas with new ones, but the new ideas are as contaminated as the old ones, because they originate from the same source. The inner anarchy we need is a change in source.

To whom or what do we turn? We have been searching for answers, but the only source of knowledge that we appear to have access to comes from outside ourselves.

But who or what out there can rescue us and place us on the right path? Religion invented a story about an all-powerful and all-knowing God up in the sky that is not real. Science, politics, and all our other societal institutions have been tainted with the same flawed understanding.

Is there anything else? What other source is there? Who or what out there can rescue us from this mess?

The truth is that—even with our best efforts—no one and nothing out there can save us. It is impossible to fix ourselves with our current way of thinking. We are doomed!

Our mistake is that we keep searching for answers out there. Perhaps we have been looking in the wrong place? Maybe the answer has always been right under our noses and we haven't realized it. Maybe there is a power within us that can do it. A higher dimension?

CHAPTER FOUR

*The world Jesus was intimately tied to and operated
within was a different world than planet Earth
and all its underlying premises.*

THERE IS ANOTHER WORLD.

Science tells us there are at least one hundred billion galaxies in the universe. A galaxy is full of stars: our sun is just one of at least one thousand million stars in our own Milky Way galaxy, and each of those stars could have their own planetary system. In our solar system, Earth is the third planet from the sun. But none of this relates to the kind of world to which I am referring.

We've also heard the statement, "They're living in their own little world," describing someone's mental or introspective reality—someone who is daydreaming or lost in deep thought or concentration.

The world I am speaking of is different from all that. It is real, but it is not located in space and does not have any physical attributes like size or weight. It is a dimension that exists within us, a consciousness, but it is not accessed through the normal reasoning and workings of the mind. That mindset has been trained from birth to relate us to the material world we presently understand. That is the only world we know.

Or is it?

We actually touch a higher dimension quite regularly. It's something that bubbles up from within us. We experience it as sudden, dramatic-breakthrough-type, deep feelings that open up within us. You have had these deep feelings before in the simplest moments. It can be triggered by viewing a beautiful sunset, listening to moving music, being in love, or even having a religious conversion. It is something we connect with when our normal mind lets its guard down and we respond to feelings deep down within us.

I'm an outdoors person, and I've often had these inner experiences while walking along the ocean shoreline or taking in the view from a scenic mountain overlook. The deep feelings were so powerful that I wanted to go back to those same places to feel them again. But were these deep feelings predicated upon my being in a certain place?

At times, these deep feelings have opened up when I was connected with others in a bond of love and altruism. After a tornado wiped out several of our nearby neighborhoods, many of us who had not previously met voluntarily joined together to help clear out rubble and offer assistance to folks in need. We all felt those deep, uplifting feelings as we helped others in crisis. The experience was so powerful that some of us stay in contact with each other to this day. It was more than just feeling good because we helped someone; there was an experience of oneness that we all felt. It was a very real and powerful feeling of being one family.

Could it be possible that these feelings of oneness are actually sitting in us all the time, running through us all?

I have had those same family-type feelings at the strangest times. I recently felt it when I was having a brief conversation with the cashier at the grocery store. I can't explain why, but those oneness feelings opened up inside me. We connected with each other from that deeper source within us both. It was an uplifting experience.

We tend to equate these inner experiences with whatever triggers them. We want to go back to the ocean, be with that particular person or group of people, listen to that same music, or involve ourselves with some activity that resembles the scenario in which we experienced those uplifting feelings. But consider the possibility that those deep feelings do not originate from a world outside of you, but from a world within you.

Regardless of whatever triggers those feelings in those moments, everything else fades away and you feel something powerful open up deep inside you—a bridge to that other world. It has more substance than a mental connection. These "bridging" sensations are in a different dimension from our daily thoughts and emotions that are continually changing. The deep feelings I'm talking about are more substantial and powerful. They have an uplifting quality to them. They are often accompanied by homecoming sensations in which you feel connected to and nestled in a sweet, freeing, almost intoxicating oneness or harmony or beauty. Those deep feelings open you to a reality that is more real than anything you can see with your eyes, touch with your hands, or think in your head. It is not restricted by the limitations of time and space. It is as if you have connected with a whole new mind. In fact, the minute you start reasoning too much about it with your normal mind, you lose it.

I know you—like me—have experienced this. And like me in the past, when you did, you probably brushed it off or didn't give it much credibility, heading back into your old, familiar mental-reasoning mind. It's easy to ignore that connected feeling, especially if you have been influenced by the religious mindset, which teaches that what you feel inside is suspect and cannot be trusted. Most of us have heard the Jeremiah 17:9 passage that says the "heart is deceitful above all things." What you probably didn't hear is that the word "heart" is not referring to your innermost deep feelings, but the reasoning of the mind.

These are two very distinct and different worlds. In John 17, Jesus identified these two worlds when he said, "I am in this world but not of this world." The first "world" Jesus was referring to, using the Greek word cosmos, involves all the attitudes, beliefs, and mindsets that are governing this planet. These include not only secular mindsets but also religious ones—both are fundamentally based on the same logic.

Jesus said he was living "in" that world but was not "of" that world. In other words, the world Jesus was intimately tied to and operated within was a different world than planet Earth and all its underlying premises. He was able to connect to a different source. Jesus often spoke of this higher world by using the designation of the "kingdom of God" or the "kingdom of heaven." The word "heaven" literally means "to be lifted up, to be elevated, happiness, eternity and power." The phrase "the kingdom" means "the authority." People often asked Jesus why they could not find this "authority." He told them it was a dimension within themselves. They would find it there! Jesus said, "The kingdom of heaven is within you" (Luke 17:21).

Finding the kingdom of heaven inside ourselves is a difficult pill to swallow. Why? Because one of the central tenets of the ideologies, belief systems, and mindsets that rule over us is to externalize all authority for our lives. Who or what determines your personal worth, value, and significance? According to our belief systems, the correct answer includes the approval and admiration of others, your financial status, your possessions, and your achievements. Who or what should impart and guide your spiritual path and reality? Again, our belief systems direct us to look outside ourselves—God up above, the institutional church, the Bible, religious dogma, academia, and any number of anointed gurus and highly acclaimed worldly experts.

The only place this externalization path leads to is the bankrupt, powerless mentality that keeps us locked in a dying world in continual conflict with itself.

Jesus called us to look inside. Only there can we begin the inner anarchy.

CHAPTER FIVE

Jesus was an inner anarchist. His central message was that another world was waiting to be born.

JESUS CHALLENGED PEOPLE TO LAY DOWN, WALK AWAY, AND STOP PARTICIPATING IN THE RELIGIOUS AND WORLDLY IDEAS THAT RULED OVER THEM.

He challenged people to find heaven inside themselves.

Jesus drew a line in the sand, clarifying the whole matter with a simple choice: either follow the external worldly and religious kingdom and all its values, beliefs, narratives, mindsets, and ideologies OR turn within and follow the authority inside you. He said it wasn't possible to serve two masters. We would simply compromise them both.

On one occasion, recorded in Matthew 24, some of Jesus' followers were having a discussion about the grandeur of the Jewish temple. One said, "This is a beautiful temple, built with the best stones. Look at the many good gifts that have been offered to God!" Jesus' responded, "The time will come when all that you see here will be destroyed. Every stone of these buildings will be thrown down to the ground. Not one stone will be left on another!"

What was Jesus talking about? A wrecking ball demolishing buildings? No. Think of the temple as the *cosmos*—the religious and worldly mindsets that rule over our world. They are all the beliefs and attitudes we carry around in our minds that block us from being free. These invisible beliefs form a powerful psychological barrier—a veil—that prevents our participation in the kingdom that Jesus spoke of. He said this "temple" will be torn down stone by stone. We now see this happening on a daily basis!

Many people want to keep one foot on the religious path and simultaneously explore a higher dimension. It's not going to happen. We have to divest ourselves of the religious way entirely. As Jesus said in Matthew 9:17, we can't pour new wine into old wineskins. It would become contaminated by the old and be useless. The message of Jesus cannot be understood in or through worldly or religious reasoning. We can't use his message to patch up and modify our present world. We need to reject where we are and start all over again from scratch. It means an inner rebirth for all of us. This puts us all on the same playing field. We are all in this together.

Jesus was an inner anarchist. His central message was that another world was waiting to be born. The people confused this message with the notion that Jesus was somehow going to physically displace the ruling regime of the day and achieve political freedom. Jesus did not advocate the expulsion of religious or worldly leaders by the sword. Instead, he told people to find liberation inside themselves and then unlock the prison cells for everyone else to break free.

While Jesus did not advocate physical violence, he also wasn't a nicely groomed Caucasian male, wandering around in a flowing white robe, offering loving feel-good teachings while holding a baby lamb in his arms. Jesus sought to overthrow the false ideologies that rule and confuse us.

Jesus was a threat to the religious and worldly ruling class who used their belief systems to rule over people. Their emphasis was on cleaning up our outer actions by laying down rules and regulations on everyone. They concentrated on policing so-called outer sinful acts with codes of conduct. Jesus, however, looked to the source of these "sinful" acts—the "sin," which is that messed-up data dominating our minds. There is a difference between sin and sinful acts. Sinful acts are the result of "sin," and it is "sin" that needed cleaning up! He took on the religious establishment and the worldly authorities of his day. He told them that they may look good on the outside, but that didn't fool him. They were loaded to hilt on the inside with all sorts of diabolical wickedness and treachery that Jesus called them out for, which eventually cost him his life.

When Jesus cleansed the temple, he kicked over chairs, upturned tables, and drove out the money changers. That is the kind of inner anarchy we need, symbolizing what has to be done inside us—a massive spring cleaning from top to bottom. Clean out our temples! Living inside our heads are all those worldly and religious lies and deceptions that have enslaved us and convinced us of their authority. They are constantly doing business in our heads—controlling us, limiting us, sabotaging us, condemning us, and accusing us. We need to get rid of them. They are driving us crazy. They just use us and eventually kill us. We can no longer be a home for them. Upturn those tables! Toss those chairs!

Consider one chair in particular to toss: our present human reality and how it does not line up with Jesus' promise of a new world. We try every conceivable theological explanation to avoid admitting that something is desperately wrong, continuing to rely on some God in the sky who is going to bail us out.

In many respects we have never progressed past the most primitive notions of a God out there, somewhere up in the sky. It is the way our minds have been trained to think. That training encourages all our belief systems—worldly and religious—to become "deities," ruling us from somewhere "out there" in the netherworld of our imaginations.

That training in the Christian religion has been the immovable stone, sealing off the secret within us that Jesus taught would save our world. Those who cling to that training stand in the doorway, not entering in themselves and blocking everyone else who is wishing to enter. This is tragic.

It is time to rebel and find that new world. Listen to that world. Follow that world. Express that world. It's a very different world than this one, and it will open up a whole new reality if we will only begin to trust it. This is what Jesus taught, what he lived for, and what he died for. Jesus offered hope to anyone who wanted to discover that new world: "Seek and you shall find, knock and it shall be opened to you" (Matt. 7:7).

But how do we make the change?

There are conditions to be met, but they are not difficult. It is only our ignorance that has been in the way. First we need to throw away our allegiance to this present world. We cannot continue trying to serve two authorities. We will never fix this broken world the way we have been trying, regardless of how noble our intentions might be. The ideologies, mindsets, and belief systems that are ruling our world are killing us. We owe it nothing. Its day is done.

For two thousand years, the Christian religion has been trying to drag Jesus into all the worldly and religious mindsets that are powerless and lead nowhere. Maybe it's time that we actually do what Jesus instructed—leave this world behind and follow him.

Jesus clearly stated what was required to leave our old order behind and birth a new world. We just haven't had the ears to hear.

CHAPTER SIX

It's a daunting proposition to dump the only world we've ever known to enter a new dimension we're just discovering.

JESUS DID NOT TEACH THAT HEAVEN IS FOUND IN THE AFTERLIFE.

His central message was that the kingdom of heaven is present in this life. The other and equally significant part of his message involved meeting a condition for entering into that higher dimension. That condition is repentance. The primary message of Jesus was "Repent, for the kingdom of heaven has come."

You might be thinking that if this were true, we certainly would have heaven by now from the full load of repentance throughout the ages. The central teaching of religion is God's judgment, which has made us all feel guilty and condemned. Even today, this world is filled with people who feel regret, contrition, and shame for the countless ways we've been told that we fall short of God's holiness. So, if the condition for entering the kingdom of heaven were that kind of shame-soaked repentance, we all would have arrived by now. There would be no one here!

The misteaching of what Jesus meant by "repent" has kept people circling around in that *cosmos* of false beliefs and mindsets that lead nowhere.

The word Jesus actually used was *metanoia*. *Meta* means "beyond or outside," while *noia* means "understanding." *Noia* is derived from the Greek *nous*, which means "our minds." In practical terms, *metanoia* means to "change the way we use our minds"—to think beyond the

31

normal limits of the way we have been taught to reason. It implies that we haven't been using our minds correctly. An example of this *metanoia* principle would be metaphysics. As mentioned, "meta" means outside or beyond, so metaphysics means outside the normal limits of physics. Likewise, *metanoia* is a spirit awareness that is beyond the normal reasoning of the mind, which is trained from birth to focus on our world. True *metanoia* is referencing our higher mind—the spirit.

The original *metanoia* meaning was lost by the use of the words "repent" and "repentance." *Repentance* comes to English from the old French word *repentir*, meaning "to feel regret for sins and crimes." *Repentir* came from the Latin words *penitire* (to regret) and *poenitire* (to make sorry). It is the root for "penitentiary," "penitent," and "penance" and related to "pain."

Using this understanding of "repent" perverted the true "gospel" (good news), corrupting Jesus' central message into something like, "Feel guilt, sorrow, regret, and pain because the kingdom of heaven is at hand!"

Seriously? Does that sound like good news to you?

Taking what Jesus meant by *metanoia*, you could restate Jesus' central message as follows: "The dimension and authority of heaven are here now, but it's going to require you to shift from your typical way of reasoning to an inner awareness of the Spirit inside you."

God is Spirit. That Spirit is the source of life, freedom, harmony, power, and well-being. That Spirit is within you. It's not located outside of you somewhere up in the sky; it is inside you—inside everyone! People have a hard time accepting that anything good, powerful, credible, or trustworthy could be inside them, because religion has convinced people that they are bad, powerless, and corrupt within themselves. This is a lie. Jesus never taught this.

The reasoning of our minds keeps us locked inside the powerless ideas, beliefs, mindsets, and ideologies of the *cosmos*. But when we turn to the deep feelings that bubble up from the life-giving Spirit within us, we are accessing and operating within a very different, powerful dimension—and this needs investigating. All those Father-like loving, forgiving, and protecting attributes that religion taught us to associate with a God located up in the sky are qualities of the life-giving Spirit within us. The power to save our world and create a new order is not up in the sky but inside ourselves. We are carrying it around daily.

Metanoia involves changing our allegiance. Until we know something different, people by default will follow the spirit of the times, which are all those faulty *cosmos* beliefs and mindsets that rule us from inside our minds. Jesus called for people to turn away from the spirit of the times and turn toward the Spirit of their inner depths to access the authority of heaven within us.

As discussed in chapter 4, Jesus distinguished between these two dimensions when he said, "You are from below; I am from above. You are of this world; I am not of this world." Time and time again, Jesus pointed out that there are two different dimensions to operate in. These two dimensions represent what we commonly refer to as "heaven" and "earth." There is a clear demarcation between the two. They have completely different properties or attributes. Jesus' message was about bringing the attributes and power of heaven to earth. What confuses things for us is how our mind separates these dimensions into locations and time slots. Our mind tells us that earth is down here and now, and heaven is up there and later. We have split our current world into a heaven mentality and an earth mentality, when they are really both the same power—the lower *cosmos* reasoning!

Jesus proposed something different: heaven, as a living dimension, is inside us right now, but we are never going to find or access it through the reasoning of the natural mind. It's turning to a different source, the life-giving Spirit within us that has always been there. Trusting the Spirit within was an unfamiliar, unpopular paradigm shift in Jesus' time and continues to be so today. Christianity teaches hard against this thinking. We are told we are all "sinners"—inherently bad and evil to the core.

To approach this change in thinking, imagine a kitchen cupboard with a red cup and a blue cup. Let's say every day, whenever you need a drink, you reach for the red cup. Many times throughout each day you reach for the red cup. Weeks, months, and years go by, and you keep reaching for the same red cup over and over and over and over again. It becomes an ingrained habit.

Now think of that red cup as the reasoning of the mind and all those false beliefs, mindsets, and ideologies. Countless times throughout each day, we have made a habit of operating within the dimension of the mind's warped reasoning and false ideas. We have made this choice so many times that it has become an ingrained way of approaching our lives and our world. What's in that red cup isn't going to work and never has. What's in that red cup is killing us. What's in that red cup assures that we are doomed.

Jesus' message was "Start reaching for the blue cup." *Metanoia* means choosing a different cup—accessing a different source for how we operate in this world. That source is the life-giving Spirit within us, a whole new consciousness which bubbles up inside us through our deep feelings. It's that dimension we have felt in those moments in which something real and powerful has opened up inside. It's not thinking with our minds; it's thinking in and through those deep feelings. While it still involves the use of the mind, our open minds, our thoughts are produced from those deep feelings rather than by that old mental reasoning.

It's a daunting proposition to dump the only world we've ever known to enter a new dimension we're just discovering. But Jesus en-

couraged us with these words: "Fear not, little children. I have over-
come the world (*cosmos*)" (Luke 12:32). In place of the corrupt *cosmos*,
he offers a good gift: "It is your Father's good pleasure to give you the
kingdom" (John 16:33).

CHAPTER SEVEN

*It is not the physical or bodily Jesus who is the messiah
who will save the world, but the presence
that filled Jesus and fills us too.*

CHRISTIANITY TEACHES THAT JESUS IS THE SAVIOR OF THE WORLD AND WILL ESTABLISH HIS REIGN ON EARTH.

Most Christians don't question this premise. But why hasn't this happened yet? As the teaching goes, the messiah has already come: he was born in Bethlehem, died and was resurrected to heaven, and plans on returning. But why the 2,000-year delay? The world waited long enough for Jesus to come the first time, why should we be put off for thousands of more years and suffering before our salvation is fully manifested? Religious scholars and leaders proclaim that Jesus' return is a futuristic physical event in which he will come from above and set everything right. We are told this assuredly will happen one day, but the right time has not yet come.

What's important to know about the above narrative is that we made this up! We've had this story for the past two thousand years because we operated within our faulty mental reasoning and worldly logic that tie us to an earthly physical world, which corrupted the spiritual message of Jesus. This is not even a terribly inventive story. The idea of a Sky God and a savior coming down from the sky to save the world is a recurring theme that has persisted since the most primitive religious thinking.

The Christian religion has concocted a story about Jesus that is a grave distortion of the truth, blocking the "return" he promised. This confusion stretches all the way back to the specific details about the people and places surrounding Jesus' birth. The problem lies in how these details have been interpreted and applied to Jesus. The faulty reasoning that the Christian religion has perpetuated through the ages is that Jesus himself—the physical person Jesus—is the messiah and that the salvation of the world is going to happen through specific actions that this physical Jesus is going to take when he bodily returns to earth.

The reality of the situation is that the salvation of the world is never going to happen through the physical Jesus because that Jesus is dead. Jesus never taught that the critical salvific event was the resurrection of his corpse, and there is evidence that the earliest Christians did not hold this view but believed in a spiritual resurrection. There is a well-documented mystical tradition of people seeing Jesus in visions and dreams, which was much later corrupted by the growing legend of a bodily resurrection. The apostle Paul never mentions Jesus being resurrected in the flesh. He never mentions empty tombs, physical appearances, or the ascension of Jesus into heaven afterward.

The first-century cosmological view of the world involved a three-storied universe: humankind lives on earth, believed to be at the center of the universe; above earth, God's home is in heaven; and below the earth is the underworld of demons and hell. Within this understanding of the universe, an oral tradition developed that said Jesus descended into the underworld or hell, then ascended to heaven to "sit at the right hand of God." The Apostles' Creed, widely used by many Christian denominations, states that Jesus "descended into hell" and "ascended to heaven."

But our knowledge of the universe has changed. The three-storied view that locates heaven above the earth and hell below it is no longer considered a reasonable way of understanding our universe. The Scriptures say that God is spirit, and we know that statements such as Jesus "sitting at the right hand of God" cannot mean that Jesus and God are literally sitting side by side in two chairs. Such statements are pointing to the spiritual reality that the Spirit of Jesus and the "Father" are one. They are simply different expressions of the exact same Spirit.

So how are we to understand the two brief references to the bodily ascension of Jesus in the gospels (Luke 24:50-53, Mark 16:19) and the more detailed account in Acts 1:9-11? Or for that matter, what are we to make of the accounts of Jesus' bodily post-resurrection appearances?

There is no refuting the Bible's account of Jesus' death by crucifixion, which is collaborated by other historical records. It seems a bit odd, however, that if such an extraordinary event took place—that a body resurrected itself after three days, then wandered about in a physical form for a number of days before being lifted up into the sky—no further record of it exists in historical documents.

It is well known that there was an oral tradition passed along by the first Christians, affirming the significance of the truth that Jesus bore witness to and demonstrated. But those understandings would have been related through their model of a three-storied universe. In this model, for Jesus to have dealt the final blow against evil, he would've had to descend into the underworld, where evil powers and energies were thought to originate. And for Jesus to make good on all his promises of triumph and salvation, the model would require Jesus to ascend above the earth into heaven to signify his power and authority.

The oral tradition also included numerous stories of people filled with hope and empowered by a spiritual reality that became very real to them after Jesus' death. The Gospels have many different and conflicting accounts of people having encounters with Jesus after his death. Two issues complicate matters further: none of these accounts were recorded by the people who had these experiences, and the experiences were recorded 70-100 years after their supposed occurrence. However, to merely pass these accounts off as fabrications is not appreciating the powerful reality people were experiencing at the time, let alone others trying to sort through them centuries later.

Even Paul, who wrote the bulk of the New Testament, never alludes to any post-resurrection bodily appearances of Jesus. Instead, in 1 Corinthians 15:45 he refers to Jesus as a "life-giving Spirit," which is entombed in us!

The salient point here is that his Spirit is alive. If you read the Gospels carefully, you will discover that Jesus never claimed that he was the messiah or would save the world in the way the Christian religion teaches. Instead he pointed us toward the Spirit—the same life-giving one that was in him and that he demonstrated. He stated that his authority was not derived from this physical world. Instead, he taught people to recognize a higher spiritual presence within themselves. It is not the physical or bodily Jesus who is the messiah who will save the world, but the presence that filled Jesus and fills us too. The Spirit saves. That is what he was teaching. There dwells our savior in us! It is not Jesus in the sky but "Christ in you, the hope of glory" (Colossians 1:27).

Jesus often spoke of the necessity of his death, which upset his closest followers. Jesus explained that his death was a necessary step to shift their attachment from the physical Jesus to his Spirit—that higher spiritual presence inside them. Unfortunately, the Christian religion has failed to make this shift; they pay homage and place the focus on the physical Jesus but have not turned toward or manifested that higher spiritual presence within them.

Christians typically interpret much of the Bible literally or through the filter of their particular cosmos, carnal-minded reasoning. This is also true of the biblical writers. Contrary to what some people are taught, those who wrote the scriptures were not put in some divine trance so that their writings would be clear of all outside influences. They would have had an understanding or revelation from the Spirit within them, but this didn't happen in a vacuum. They would have related their insights to the physical world and their religion as they had been taught to understand them at the time. All ancient biblical texts have a primitive or original meaning that relates to their original historical context—their culture and their cosmos.

Religion has often created doctrines out of the particular interpretations of biblical writers who were, as we are, affected by their times. However, the things that we have always accepted as doctrine may mean something quite different than what we have been led to believe. We have to trace the writers' words back to their source to get the true understanding. That source is in us—not in a book! Jesus said it was the Spirit within us that would guide us in all truth (John 16:13).

If one strips away worldly logic and reasoning, some of the key biblical passages related to Jesus take on a whole new meaning. For example, an ancient biblical prophecy speaks of a great liberating power and messiah that would arise out of Bethlehem. The actual passage is in Micah 5:2-4. The prophet Micah, who lived some 2,700 years ago, had a Spirit awareness of a messiah coming, but he would have struggled to fit this realization into how he understood his present world.

Micah's prophecy states:

> Bethlehem Ephrathah, you are one of the smallest towns in Judah, but out of you I will bring a ruler for Israel, whose family line goes back to ancient times. So the Lord will abandon his people to their enemies until the one who is to give birth has her son. Then his fellow countrymen who are in exile will be reunited with their own people. When he comes he will rule his people with the strength that comes from the Lord and with the majesty of the Lord God himself. His people will live in safety because people all over the earth will acknowledge his greatness, and he will bring peace.

Christian clergy use this well-known prophecy to support the divine authenticity of the birth of Jesus. It is bandied around the world with great rejoicing at countless Christmas services.

But let's think about this. Why the celebration? This prophecy has obviously not yet been fulfilled. One could hardly claim that people all over the earth live in safety and that peace reigns. If it had been fulfilled by the physical birth of Jesus in the actual town of Bethlehem—if indeed the messiah had come in that scenario—then our world would not be in the mess and misery that it is in right now. That is logical, isn't it?

But if you take another look at this prophesy and the events surrounding the birth of Jesus, we find some clues that point to the true messiah.

Just what does "Bethlehem Ephrathah" mean in the Micah passage? The Hebrew translates it as "an ever-increasing fruitful family, or house, that brings forth food, especially bread that prevails and overcomes."

Does that sound like a little town near Jerusalem to you?

It sounds to me more like a group of people—a family, an atmosphere—that brings forth a sustenance in the world that is powerful and triumphant. Who would this family be? Us! And what is this bread that we bring into the world? It is the "living bread," which is the life-giving Spirit within us. In other words, there is a "heavenly" Bethlehem—a spiritual dimension inside us—and from this inner Bethlehem, a powerful and triumphant reality is to be birthed out of us into the world.

The physical birth of Jesus twenty centuries ago was pointing toward a spiritual reality that is to be born out of our hearts to save the world. It's often difficult for Christians to grasp this because they have been trained to focus on the physical Jesus rather than the Spirit of Jesus. According to mainstream Christian teaching, the physical Jesus resurrected from the grave, currently has a corporeal existence up above in heaven, and one day will bodily return to earth to save the world. Jesus, however, instructed his followers to be looking not for him but for his Spirit, his presence, guiding, teaching, comforting, and empowering them from the inside. This Spirit has been entombed in us for centuries and we never knew it! We were taught our messiah would come down from the sky, and that has been our stumbling block.

Other details about the Jesus story also point to the identity of this promised messiah within us. Jesus insisted that he was intimately connected to David, who died about a thousand years before Jesus was born. Jesus stated that he was a descendant from the line of David. Jesus' birth town, Bethlehem, was also called the "city of David." Jesus even went as far as claiming that he was the "son of David." The birth story of Jesus has Mary betrothed to Joseph, but Jesus identified himself as a descendant of David. This is clarified at the outset of Matthew's Gospel. The genealogy of Jesus is established and he is referred to as the "son of David."

The name David means "beloved"—a state of being covered and enveloped by love. Hmm. So Jesus is the son of this all-encompassing reality of love? And this love is his "Father"? And so this spirit of "David" the "Father" of the "Messiah" is influencing us?

Yes! We have touched and experienced this dimension within ourselves. It came in the form of a powerful and triumphant feeling or sensation of being loved. It's that homecoming and lifting-up experience inside us when we turn to our deeper feelings. Many have experienced this "Father" within them. Christians do too, but they think it comes from out of the sky! The scriptures say, "God is love" (1 John 4:8). Not that false "God" up in the sky, but the life-giving Spirit who resides inside us.

CHAPTER EIGHT

*The birth of a new world will come when we are
drawn together by those love sensations deep within us.*

WELL THEN, IF "DAVID" IS THE FATHER OF THIS COMING MESSIAH BEING FORMED WITHIN US, THEN WHO IS THE MOTHER?

Yes, you guessed it—it would have to be "Mary." However, Mary is not the serene and submissive one we see portrayed on Christmas cards. Oh no! The New Testament "Mary" is the Greek rendering of the Hebrew *Marion*. It means "bitter rebellion."

"Mary" is that spirit of anarchy—the need to rebel against the belief systems that have been dumped on us and led us astray. Can you now see? That is "Mary," the mother of the messiah, within us! That is the anarchy that we have been talking about that is so necessary. That is the messiah's mom! No mom, then no messiah!

Mary was betrothed to Joseph. "Joseph" means "to add, to increase." The Spirit of Joseph, when applied to the particulars of the birth of Jesus, increases and broadens the revelation beyond its literal dimensions, giving our reasoning a multidimensional heavenly lift!

Glimmers of the real "messiah" became evident in the Western world about fifty years ago when "David" was crossed with "Mary," rebelling against the establishment and tradition. The world was struggling to give birth but didn't understand what was happening to it. This was when younger people began to break from the system, questioning the ruling ideologies of the day, and came together in genuine love and peace.

It was the '60s—the flower people and the hippie movement. People danced around, had a good time, and expressed these questioning sentiments through music. "Mary" was beginning to rebel against the world and turn toward her true husband, "David."

"David" was a shepherd boy who courageously protected his flock. He was raised in "Bethlehem" (David's city). He loved music and "Saul," the disobedient first king of the Jews, who turned to witches for spiritual advice and summoned "David" to play a lyre to appease his tormented soul. Music has an uplifting quality to it, which is why it is typically a central component of most Christian worship gatherings. Music has always related well to me. I've always found music to be an effective way to begin to touch and energize heart feelings in people.

A "wedding" was beginning to take place in the '60s, and the old wine was being replaced with the new. This "wedding at Cana" in which the old ceremonial water was turned into a top vintage wine was documented as being the first miracle of Jesus. This was symbolic of a spiritual wedding that would miraculously transform the old order into something new.

During the '60s, many sacred cows and traditional values were dismantled, but no one knew where to go from there. As the movement receded, it became more extreme and fantastical, slipping back under the control of the *cosmos*. It became more gritty, aggressive, frustrated, fragmented . . . and stoned! I have talked with people who spoke of experiencing a tremendous lift during that period and they wonder where it all went wrong. To them, the deterioration of the movement was tragic. They speak of an energy of love, authenticity, togetherness, and harmony that connected people together as never before. To them, it showed the possibilities that a whole new world could have opened up.

This manifestation kept evolving right through to the "Jesus people" and then into the charismatic renewal, which began to reveal and identify the life-giving Spirit that was behind it all. However, religious belief systems, promoted by Bible experts bent on building their own kingdoms, quickly intervened and blocked the Spirit, forcing us back into the old order Bible based intellectual order.

Through a lack of understanding of what was occurring and its potential, many of the folks from the '60s gradually and reluctantly worked themselves back into the system. Many became "successful" and tried to morph into the world, but feel like they never did what they really wanted to do and now express a sense of emptiness about life and their shallow relationships.

The true messiah is born out of the joining of love and rebellion against the old systems. The true messiah is a powerful reality that is born out of a family of people. Where is this true messiah coming from? Us!

But for this messiah to be released, we also need "Mary." We need rebellion! There has to be inner anarchy. We can no longer serve two masters. We must rebel against that old, external, make-believe, slave-driving "God" and the entire mindset and reasoning that go along with it.

Jesus said, "I am in this world but not of this world." In other words, Jesus was saying, "I am a real person living on a real earth, but I do not operate under the premises of those religious and worldly ideas." When he spoke of his "return," he spoke of his "presence" coming. "Where two or three are gathered together 'in my nature'"—connected to his Spirit—"there I am in the midst of them" (Matt. 18:20). He also alluded to his return initially being like a thief in the night (Matt. 24:42-44). Have we been missing something? Is this happening right now?

The birth of a new world will come when we are drawn together by those love sensations deep within us, and we stand together in rebellion against the mindsets and ideologies of this world. From this, a whole new persona will emerge. Starting among a few people, it will be a "togetherness" that brings forth real food that stands firm and overcomes.

This new nature or personality will be revealed by the way we speak. We will be talking from a new source of logic, and when we do, things will start to happen. We will see real miracles.

Outbreaks of the Spirit have been recorded throughout history. Most Christian denominations began after being triggered by such events. But much like what happened in the '60s, these occurrences are misunderstood and are soon conformed into those familiar worldly and religious mindsets. But that light cannot be extinguished; it is intensifying, coming out into the open with a new boldness and resistance to being turned back. People are opening up and speaking more freely and expressing their feelings. The light is coming!

The disciples were told to stop staring into the clouds, waiting for the return of Christ. "Why do you stare up into the sky?" they were asked. Jesus was not going to come back down from the sky. Instead, they were told that Jesus would return in the same way that he departed (Acts 1:11). What way was that? The scriptures speak of Jesus' departure from the world as a "lifting up" into the atmosphere. Jesus spoke of his death as a new beginning—a "lifting up"—specifically, a lifting up of the Spirit in each of us. The "return of Christ"—the savior of the world—is the Spirit released and "lifted up" in and out of each of us. This creates a wonderful, powerful, loving, joyful atmosphere where anything becomes possible.

We are not going to get anywhere until we start trusting what is within us. You are afraid and doubt what lies deep within you, but what lies deep within you is your salvation and the salvation of the world. We are the "Bethlehem"—the family and household who must birth into the world that living bread and triumphant Spirit that overcomes, prevails, and makes all things new.

But don't forget "Mary." Without her, there is no messiah. And we desperately need one!

CHAPTER NINE

*Truth is simply speaking from a pure heart, which we
can all do if we connect with the Spirit of Jesus within us.*

WHAT WAS THE FOCUS OF JESUS' MINISTRY ON EARTH?

Time and time again, Jesus stated that he came for the "lost sheep of the house of Israel." Of all the people scattered around the globe to whom Jesus could have come, the Jewish people were the ones chosen. Jesus had no real focus on the irreligious Gentiles or other so-called heathens around the world. He wasn't out to convert them. Instead he came to be born into the most religiously inclined group of people on the face of this planet. If he wished to be killed for arguing theology, then he couldn't choose a better scenario! Just what was the purpose of that?

What was his mission?

We get a clue when Jesus was asked almost the same question by Pilate. After being delivered to Pilate by the religious Jewish leaders to be executed for blaspheming their God (and claiming he was God), Jesus told Pilate that he was a king but his kingdom was *not of this physical world!* If it were, then naturally enough, he would have armies fighting for him so he wouldn't get handed over to the Jews.

Then Jesus said to Pilate, "You say correctly that I am a king. For this I have been born, and for this I have come into the world, to testify [to bear witness, to demonstrate] to the truth. Everyone who is of the truth hears my voice" (John 18:37).

So the mission of Jesus of two thousand years ago was to demonstrate a higher truth—a truth not of this world.

Pilate asked, "What is truth?"

Apparently Jesus never responded, but Pilate inadvertently answered his own question when he said to the Jews, "I find no guile in him."

Truth is simply speaking from a pure heart, which we can all do if we connect with the Spirit of Jesus within us.

In contrast to the pure heart Pilate encountered in Jesus are the religious leaders' hearts, filled with hypocrisy, pride, and self-righteousness, driven by distorted "God" beliefs. But Jesus did not back down in confronting them. In fact, Jesus faced the religious establishment head-on, and it wasn't pretty. Jesus said his kingdom—his authority—was not sourced in this world. And he accused the religious elites of building a kingdom sourced from their relationship with the world, the *cosmos*, which resulted in oppressing people in the name of "God." This "God" had been fashioned from the beliefs, attitudes, legends, and myths picked up over the centuries. Jesus called their "God" an impostor, a liar, and a murderer—even the Devil! There was no truth in that "God"!

In Matthew 23, Jesus delivers a scathing rebuke of the religious establishment in the form of seven woes and throws in a few nasty terms to describe the practitioners for good measure. He condemned these self-proclaimed "men of God" for operating with a false, baseless claim of divine authority. He characterizes their entire religious operation as a spiritually dead and bankrupt farce, led by frauds and swindlers.

Why would Jesus do this? Clearly, taking on the religious elites so fervently was a guarantee of his death. If Jesus had backed off or toned it down, he might have had more years left to share his truth with those who had ears to hear. Why was this confrontation so important to Jesus? Why would he continue a fight that put him at grave risk and ultimately cost him his life?

Jesus made it clear that he came first and foremost for his own people—the Jews. They were the "chosen ones" to be "the light of the world"—called to save the world—but they were doing it all wrong! Jesus was not concerned with bothering the consciousness of millions and millions of other people around the globe. He said he came for the "lost sheep of the house of Israel" (Matt. 15:24). Notice that Jesus described his people as "lost." Rather than being the light of the world, they went around fanatically converting people to their corrupted religion. Jesus said, "You travel over land and sea to win a single convert, and when you have succeeded, you make them twice as much a child of hell as you are" (Matt. 23:15).

If you closely read the seven woes that Jesus leveled against the religious establishment, you will see that what he loathed most about the situation is how they were binding people to a dead and powerless religion, effectively preventing them from entering the kingdom of God. Jesus says, "Woe to you, teachers of the law and Pharisees, you hypocrites! You shut the door of the kingdom of heaven in people's faces. You yourselves do not enter, nor will you let those enter who are trying to" (Matt. 23:13).

Jesus could not turn away from his confrontation with these religious leaders, because they were the stumbling block that had to be removed for people to enter the kingdom of God within them and be free. These leaders were perpetuating the *cosmos* beliefs and mindsets that kept people all wrapped up in this earthly world, unaware of the heavenly world inside them. They kept driving people to bow down and worship a make-believe, useless God who, they said, lived somewhere out there. They erected buildings with steeples pointing up to the sky all over the place! (Hmm . . . sounds like the Bible Belt to me!) By promoting this thinking and focusing everyone in the wrong direction, they were standing in the way of the salvation of the whole world—the release of the true messiah, straining to be birthed from out of the people.

Jesus points out that they were preventing the people from entering the kingdom of heaven and that they were not going to enter that kingdom themselves. They were the priesthood but were not doing what they were commissioned to do. First and foremost, Jesus was offering freedom and the kingdom of God to his own people. But they would have none of it. They were too stiff-necked in their religious ways to listen. Over and over, Jesus challenged them to wake up. On one occasion he told them that their devotion to the scriptures was useless: "You search the scriptures, for you believe they give you eternal life. And the scriptures point to me! Yet you won't come to me so that I can give you this life eternal" (John 5:39-40).

People often equate the parable of the lost sheep as referring to the irreligious, "sinful," and "depraved" people of the world that the religious establishment self-righteously judged and condemned. But it's clear from what Jesus' stated about his mission that the "lost sheep" were these proud, corrupt religious leaders. Turning one of them toward the truth was worth a heavenly celebration, because that meant one less person blocking the way for others. And the fruit from that person's ministry could change the lives of thousands.

So who are those chosen people today? Who are those who are called to save the world? Who are the lost sheep of Israel? Isn't it obvious? It's those who preach Jesus. Those who claim to represent Jesus and his truth to the world. What Jesus is reported to have said two thousand years ago was said for today. There are a lot of lost sheep around now. They have let us and themselves down.

CHAPTER TEN

It is ironic:
the ones called to save the world
are blocking the way.

JESUS IS AS SAD AS HE IS ANGRY OVER CURRENT CHRISTIAN LEADERS' REFUSING TO LISTEN TO HIM.

It is ironic: the ones called to save the world are blocking the way. This is ridiculous! There are millions of poor, suffering people on earth who live with despair and terror, but without hope. And all the Christians can offer is a powerless gospel. That is not what Jesus preached or demonstrated. In fact, he even said his followers would do greater works than he did (John 14:12). Surely the leaders realize something is missing. Doesn't this make them consider getting back to the drawing board and rechecking their Jesus understandings?

Jesus wept over the people of Jerusalem for their unwillingness to accept what he was offering. He passionately confronted their misunderstanding of his mission, but he loved them and wanted them to enter the kingdom of God within them.

That was then and this is now, but we have the same scenario happening today. Jesus came two thousand years ago to demonstrate, testify, and bear witness to the truth, and that truth still stands. There is a heavenly Bethlehem within each of us, and the same Spirit that was in Jesus is in us—that is the true messiah that is to be birthed out of us to save the world! We are the priesthood, but instead of turning people toward the Spirit within, the Christian religion did and does the very thing Jesus exhorted his disciples not to do—build a religion around the physical human Jesus. Jesus stated unequivocally that his kingdom and authority were not rooted in this *cosmos*—the carnal and religious mental reasoning and mindsets of this world. This faulty *cosmos* thinking perpetuates the most primitive notions about God and Jesus.

Consider the *cosmos* version of the crucifixion. No physical sacrifice—animal or human—has any power to save the world that is locked under the strict limitations of time and space! It is the wrong realm. And yet the Christian religion concocted a story of the physical Jesus being crucified and punished on the cross, somehow having all our evil physical deeds dumped on him. This so-called "finished work of the cross" has been done in our current terrestrial world, even though the laws of science make it impossible for these so-called paranormal events to occur.

This "cross" doctrine relates to the false Sky God mentality. It is based on the primitive desire to appease a wrathful God up above, promoting the illogical tit (our sin) for tat (Jesus' sinless life) exchange and a pagan mentality toward God—he's angry, so offer sacrifices to calm the tyrant. This just distracts us from the fact that the real culprits driving us in all our sinful acts are the corrupted beliefs and attitudes that have been causing us grief for centuries. THAT is what Jesus came to deal with, and to do that his nature has to be inside of us. As it stands now, we have a screwed-up scenario in which the only gods that exist are those created by ourselves. They can't save anyone—nor can the physical Jesus, no matter how much we worship him! Rather than turning to his Spirit within them, the Christian leaders dragged the physical Jesus out of the grave and sent him up into the clouds to be with an all-powerful Sky God who manages human affairs and will one day send Jesus floating down from the heavens to save the world.

The Christian church has constructed a belief system that denies and twists the powerful spiritual truths that Jesus taught and lived, and in so doing has preached a powerless gospel that has led countless people into a religious maze that goes nowhere. Our colossal error was telling people that they are inherently bad, separated from God, and should not trust what is inside them.

For the past two thousand years the Christian religion has been the immovable stone that has sealed off the tomb of the eternal life-giving Spirit within us. Christian leadership can't even come to a unified agreement and oneness among themselves. Surely that fact alone gives us grounds to rethink a few things.

I was once one of those religious leaders. As I mentioned in the first chapter, I was the seminary graduate with a master of divinity degree. I was the successful senior pastor whom people turned to for truth. I was the religious leader and Bible expert whom people trusted. But I was the one who preached that powerless gospel, held up that carrot and the stick, handcuffed people to that false God, misrepresented Jesus, and misused the Bible—all the while claiming to be divinely anointed. I was sincere in doing all of these things, but I was sincerely wrong and ignorant.

This is an appeal to others out there like me. We are the "priesthood" that dropped the ball. We created quite the clusterfuck that has led people in circles for centuries. We have sufficiently buried the entire spiritual dimension that could have saved this world beneath layer upon layer of theological doctrines, worldly mindsets, and religious constructs that have no power. We have conditioned people into a dependency upon external things—Sky God (aka "Father"), the institutional Christian system (aka "church"), religious dogma (aka "Bible"), and religious gurus (aka "pastors," "authors," "spiritual leaders," and "teachers")—and have failed to connect people to the eternal, life-giving Spirit within them.

We cannot go back and undo the past, but we can courageously act now for the salvation of all humankind. We screwed up. That was then. This is now. And now we must be on the front lines, making things right.

We have to remove every stumbling block that people are tripping over every day. We need to release the Spirit of Jesus into the world. That is what we have been appointed to do.

But we have to get our act together first.

We are the priesthood called to join together and lead the way across the Jordan into the promised land. "Jordan" means "to descend—to go deeper." We can no longer foster dependency on ourselves and the programs and structures we have created; instead, we need to encourage people to go deeper inside themselves and form a partnership with the Spirit.

This task requires setting aside all our little, individual, worldly-religious-ego kingdoms and bringing people together to lift out from within us the heavenly dimension—the new Jerusalem from heaven—that Jesus said would save our world. There is no God in the sky to rescue us. Unbeknownst to us, we have been living for thousands of years in a world where no active God exists—at least not a God in the way that religious leaders have reasoned him to be. We should have recognized centuries ago that there is not some all-powerful being located beyond the clouds who has been overseeing and plotting the affairs of humankind. The God we must become aware of is the eternal life-giving Spirit that runs through all of us.

That false God of religion must be dethroned once and for all, so we can get on with a real plan of action that has power. The whole creation groans with the pains of childbirth (Rom. 8:22), waiting for us to birth and manifest the messiah out of ourselves and into this world. If we will turn people toward the Spirit within them, this will happen. The Spirit says, "Let my people go!" Forget your reputation and good standing. Stand for a new possibility, a new future, and a new opening of the Spirit in our day right now!

CHAPTER ELEVEN

*Regardless of your sincerity and good intentions,
as it now stands, you are just a pawn to an ideology
that is sealing a tragic fate for our world.*

MORE THAN 7 BILLION PEOPLE ARE ON THE PLANET, AND ABOUT 2.5 BILLION OF THEM ARE CHRISTIANS.

Christians claim to have the only-true-God connection and view themselves as the only qualified ones called to minister the truth to save humankind. They believe that privilege is theirs because they are the Bible experts. There are 41,000 different Christian denominations around the world, and close to 450,000 international missionaries mobilized abroad. The Roman Catholic Church is considered to be the largest financial power on earth. Evangelical Christianity isn't doing too shabby either. A top Christian televangelist lives in a $10 million house, another one drives a $350,000 Bentley, and several of them make more than $1 million a year. One megachurch meets in a sports stadium, draws close to 50,000 people for a worship service, and has an annual budget that exceeds $70 million. Speaking of budgets, 82 percent of the average church budget is used to cover the expense of buildings and salaries. Considering the number of people, buildings, and dollars, Christendom is quite an impressive empire on planet Earth.

But for what? What has this shiny, lucrative Christian empire actually accomplished? What do we have to show for it? We haven't made even a dent in the suffering that plagues humankind and our planet. But I'll give us one thing—you sure have to admire the sheer size of this discordant monstrosity. However, Jesus, as a homeless man with a handful of confused followers, stirred up more controversy in three years than the entire Christian church has done in three centuries. He is still being worshipped two thousand years later.

Jesus' disciples once marveled at the outer grandeur of the Jewish Temple. On the outside, the Temple looked quite impressive in worldly terms but, on the inside, it was bankrupt. The Temple leaders and the whole system was a fraudulent enterprise, mockery of the truth, and instrument of oppression and extortion among the people. Jesus said he would destroy this Temple, made with hands, and within three days build another made without hands.

That "temple" symbolically made of outer and inner courts and a holy place represents the dynamics of our world—the *cosmos*. It is a picture of our world developed from the best of our religious and secular endeavors. We have all played our various parts in the construction of this mammoth organization. Many facets of this temple of ours have to be admired. There are shows of remarkable ingenuity and brilliance. We can be amazingly clever in building and maintaining this wonderful temple. Look how we keep modifying our systems to keep things going. Problems can and do pop up endlessly from all over the place, but we somehow rise to the occasion and patch things up and keep the system running. We keep slogging on, but it is becoming clear to many that, in spite of our best efforts, the mammoth organization is leading us into disaster. It is doomed. Problems that threaten our existence are morphing and multiplying at a rate that can no longer be addressed. Total confusion is standing at the door. Our mental stability is breaking down, and it is becoming obvious that we are bluffing our way through life, hiding deep hurts and despair.

We need a true savior now! Where is that being with an unadulterated, clear-thinking mind who can put us straight? We definitely need a mind transplant, replacing our clouded one with the truth. The Christians, being the appointed priesthood, have the right to enter the inner sanctuaries on behalf of the people. They are the ones who have the authority to bring in our savior—to release that new mind buried in us. But what have they done? They have completely abused their calling. They haven't been releasing the Spirit mind; they have been blocking it!

Hits a little too close to home, doesn't it? It should. Look at the mess around us. Christians face the same difficulties as everyone else. Consider Jesus' words as relevant for the Christian establishment of today. Jesus has put us all on notice. The game is over! Done! Finished! The monstrosity—like our minds—will collapse on itself in a heap of rubble.

Come on, you Christian leaders! How often have we spent hours pontificating to the masses about how to strain out a gnat while we gulp down a huge, ole camel?

We can't just keep carrying on like this. It is time to wake up! Let's face it: the rest of the world is fed up and regards us as just a pain in the ass and a joke, yet we think we have been so smart. The truth is we have completely bastardized and ignored the nature of our true Spirit Father and imposed upon everyone a false "physical" God that we have created entirely in our image. As his representatives, we have given him a completely erroneous, nasty depiction. It is our responsibility to put things right!

Jesus said, "Why do you look at the speck of sawdust in your brother's eye and pay no attention to the plank in your own eye? How can you say to your brother, 'Let me take the speck out of your eye,' when all the time there is a plank in your own eye? You hypocrite, first take the plank out of your own eye, and then you will see clearly to remove the speck from your brother's eye" (Matt. 7:3-5).

That's the problem! Regardless of your sincerity and good intentions, as it now stands, you are just a pawn to an ideology that is sealing a tragic fate for our world. That system has no power to save anyone, including you. Millions of people are hurting, but we religious leaders are in no position to aid and support others until we get our own act together. Wake up! We are being called back. Look what we have done. We have wantonly squandered and abused what we've been given.

Take another look at this little story from two thousand years ago, written especially for our present situation. We are that son who has been given a great inheritance—the messiah within us to minister to the world—but we have squandered this gift for ourselves and others through two thousand years of worldly and religious thinking. We have partied out on it and been deceived and given the credit of those touches we have all experienced to a fabricated God who loves being worshipped and bowed and scraped to. But that "God" is really ourselves. We worship ourselves and each other—how stupid is that? We prophesy crazy things in his name. We sing songs to the damn thing! What have we been doing? Have we all gone nuts?

But none of that matters now. All that matters is that we bury all of that and turn toward home, where we have always belonged. Let the spirit of "David" (love) and the spirit of "Mary" (rebellion) guide your path forward. Regardless of how badly we messed up things, there is a loving "Father"—the eternal Spirit who runs through us all—who will run out to greet you and welcome you and celebrate. What a party! What joy! There is just so much more for us all, and it has been put squarely in our hands to administer. There is no God up there any longer to make it happen. He has just fallen down!

Can you imagine a scenario in which us religious-leader types are no longer the ones holding everyone back, but the ones out in front, leading the charge? That's our job—confronting the craziness that has been going on in that old temple! Isn't that what you truly want to do? We can do it right this time!

Imagine coming together in an atmosphere of tremendous joy and a triumphant confidence in being that family that births the true messiah-power and dimension into our world, moving from 42,000 Christian denominations to none. When people see that, millions will turn toward us in joy as a true, living savior emerges. Envision an excitement that is not about building a kingdom unto ourselves but offering the "living bread" that opens up a whole new reality for all people. The "lost sheep of Israel" finally join hands together as one for the salvation of our world.

"By this all people will know that you are my disciples, if you have love for one another" (John 13:35).

CHAPTER TWELVE

*The salvation of the world is not going to come
through the top-notch Bible scholars and head-driven
academics, but those who are uncomplicated, trusting,
and openhearted toward reaching out to truth.*

IN A MOMENT OF GREAT JOY JESUS EXPRESSED A DEEP GRATITUDE FOR THOSE WHO WILL EXPERIENCE THIS COMING TOGETHER.

He states that these things will be "hidden from the intellectuals and worldly wise and revealed to those who are as trusting as little children" (Luke 10:21). Jesus also said, "I saw Satan fall, a bolt of lightning out of the sky. See what I've given you? Safe passage as you walk on snakes and scorpions, and protection from every assault of the Enemy. No one can put a hand on you. All the same, the great triumph is not in your authority over evil, but in God's—the eternal Spirit—authority over you and presence with you. Not what you do for him but what he does for you—that's the agenda for rejoicing" (Luke 10:18-20).

He turned to his disciples and said, "Blessed are the eyes that see what you see! For I tell you that many prophets and kings desired to see what you see, and did not see it, and to hear what you hear, and did not hear it" (Luke 10:23-24).

The salvation of the world is not going to come through the top-notch Bible scholars and head-driven academics, but those who are uncomplicated, trusting, and openhearted toward reaching out to truth. Jesus challenged the religious scholars, pointing out how useless their head knowledge was. He said, "You have your heads in your Bibles constantly because you think you'll find eternal life there. But you miss the forest for the trees. These scriptures are all about me! And here I am, standing right before you, and you aren't willing to receive from me the life you say you want" (John 5:29-30). If you have never had any formal theological or Bible training but have an open and trusting heart, you are light years ahead of that crowd!

We Christians are moping around, feeling powerless and defenseless, waiting on Jesus to come swinging out of the sky to save the day. A world of suffering people are looking to us, and the best we can offer is a message that essentially says, "Be good, go to church, give your money, obey the rules, and hold out for heaven after you die." But this is not the picture that Jesus painted. Jesus described a scenario in which all the false mindsets and ideologies ruling within us and putting our world in peril are struck down and rendered toothless. That is "Satan"—that false God that we have created falling from the sky!

Just as there is no Sky God located somewhere above, neither is there a Satan as some embodiment of evil that is a literal being and actively seeking to do harm in our world. Instead, what has always been and is today are those false religious and worldly mindsets and ideologies that hold sway in people's minds and have come to do great harm and destruction by ruling over our world.

Speaking to the religious leaders in John 8:33-34, Jesus said, "Why is my language not clear to you? Because you are unable to hear what I say. You belong to your father, the devil, and you want to carry out your father's desires. He was a murderer from the beginning, not holding to the truth, for there is no truth in him. When he lies, he speaks his native language, for he is a liar and the father of lies." These leaders could not understand the truth that Jesus was teaching, not because there was some being who was entering their minds and confusing it for them, but because their minds were being held hostage to the lies and deceptions of their distorted reasoning. Jesus identified the "devil" as their false Sky

God who supposedly ruled the world with a fist of judgment and impending wrath.

Jesus says that rather than being defenseless against the power of these lies, we will operate within an atmosphere of safety, protection, and triumph. Notice that Jesus pointed out that this will not be some kind of battle waged within the *cosmos* on physical terms. When Jesus announced that the kingdom of God had come, his disciples mistakenly assumed it would be a new political regime established by the sword. Instead, Jesus said it was a kingdom to be found and birthed into the world from within them. The authority to make these kinds of sweeping changes in the world will not come in or through that *cosmos* thinking, but in and through the power and authority of that higher spiritual presence within us. Jesus said, "He who is within you (that messiah-spirit) is greater than he who is in the world (that *cosmos*-spirit)" (1 John 4:4). Change doesn't come from all the things we are going to go out and "do for God"—we've been doing that for centuries and it has not solved anything! Instead, it's what will happen when we come together as a family and bring out from within us that "living bread" that overcomes and triumphs. As Jesus said, "That's the agenda for rejoicing!"

To be that family requires a shift in consciousness—a lifting up of our minds to a different dimension. Jesus referred to this as *metanoia* (repentance) in action.

It can't happen without inner anarchy. It's not enough to stop attending church, give up your Christian beliefs, and punt on organized religion. The reasoning and mindsets that are ruling us from within are sneaky and will persist in whatever path you take after religion. You can get rid of one belief system and roll in a new one and still be operating with the same faulty underlying premises. We can't exercise our inner demons by changing the way we do things outwardly. Even modern psychology is stumped in addressing the root causes of these inner conflicts and is left to prescribe medications to curb the turmoil when they get out of hand.

Jesus and the truth he bore witness to have very little to do with the Christian religion, which is very focused on our observed outer acts—the good or bad or shades of grey in between. Jesus went past that and put the focus on what was going on inside us. That is where our problems are. Fix that and the outer will take care of itself. Christians got it backward, concentrating on the external by forcing various codes of conduct onto people. This thinking has prejudiced people against Jesus' teachings, even among those who have left Christianity behind. It's now difficult for him to get a fair shake, given what Christianity has done. People wrongly assume that Christianity accurately represents the life and teachings of Jesus. That is not true! It is a totally botched job and needs reviewing.

Jesus was a human being like you. He was a first-century Jew in ancient Palestine. We know about him today because the truth he shared distressed a deep-rooted, 4,000-year-old religion and threatened the political and societal power centers of his day. He sure raised quite a bit of hell for one guy! Ultimately, those religious and political powers conspired together to have him killed.

Why? What danger did Jesus pose to these powers that resulted in his execution?

The truth that Jesus shared and demonstrated debunked the foundational premises on which those religious and political systems were built. Jesus called for people to stop listening to them and start listening to the spirit of truth within themselves. He attacked the credibility of those systems and told people to find their authority inside themselves. Instead of a human-led society, he was advocating a world ruled by an amazing power or Spirit mind that was already within us. Jesus called it the kingdom—the authority—of heaven. Each time Jesus opened his mouth, he was pulling out another wooden Jenga block, making these religious and worldly powers vulnerable and unstable. Jesus himself was no threat—he had no position of religious or political power and wasn't campaigning to be the worldly president—but his truth made him a one-man wrecking crew.

If Jesus were alive today, that scenario would repeat itself. He would come to his people—the Christian establishment—and they would quickly discover that his truth doesn't line up with their longstanding, "orthodox," theological tradition. Protecting their church kingdoms, Christian leaders would come out with guns blazing. Like first-century Jews, they would reject Jesus, label him a heretic, characterize him as a dangerous inciter, and ostracize him. As Jesus stirred things up and more people started listening to and following him, he would become a person of interest to our worldly and political powers. The government would not allow the rebel Jesus to go on like this—it might just get people questioning their dogma and authority as well.

It's understandable why people who have shed religion are wary of anything associated with Jesus. There has been an exodus of people leaving the traditional church, repulsed by what religion has done to them. They have had enough! Anything that smacks of religion—like references to Jesus or quoted Bible verses—gets their backs up. They automatically shut off because they are fearful of being trapped again.

I certainly understand this. When I went off the grid of organized Christianity, I went through this blackout and detox period. I could not stomach anything remotely "Christian." I didn't go to church, didn't converse about God or Christianity, didn't pray, didn't read my Bible, didn't listen to "Christian music" . . . nothing! An interesting place to be for a former seminary grad and successful senior pastor. But during this season I became deeply connected with myself, others, the divine, and life itself in ways I have never experienced before when religion was running the show. This laid a new foundation for thinking about Jesus in different terms.

Many people who shed religion find their main way of retaining and expressing that feeling of freedom is to attack religious people, whereas the real religious enemy is still very much alive within them! They criticize these believers for being so dogmatic and bound up by scripture verses, whereas they are now so beautifully free and can follow their hearts. This was me. Life was good. No more guilt or the burden of religion. I could simplify everything to a belief in love. I started using an axiom, "Life is my religion." It was my way of saying that I was done with all that religious bullshit—I was simply going to find "God" in daily life and people and be an expression of acceptance, tolerance, grace, and love.

Life was sweet. I truly believed that finally I had arrived.

CHAPTER THIRTEEN

Jesus cannot save us or the world. He is dead.
But the truth he bore witness to and demonstrated
is the salvation the world is awaiting!

UNFORTUNATELY IT DIDN'T STAY LIKE THAT.

I noticed something. Despite this newfound personal freedom, the world was continuing to fall down around our ears with strife, contention, and suffering, and people were still getting sick and dying a miserable death, leaving grieving loved ones. And again, the wheels of the bus keep going round and round.

This was troubling.

Many who have left legalistic, judgmental Christianity behind have developed a more progressive, inclusive approach. They teach that what Jesus did on the cross two thousand years ago was a finished work for everyone. Nothing further needs to be done by the individual—no believing or works—we just follow our hearts and live confidently in forgiveness and sinless perfection. To them, religion is finished . . . but they will still attack the shitters out of people who insist on proclaiming it! Obviously, religious forces are still very much alive and kicking within them. And if indeed "it is finished" like they say, then a whole bunch of people never received the memo, because this world is a bloody mess! And that is two thousand years removed from the source event. How much longer do we have to wait?

What gives?

People who leave religion behind are still under the same God they had before, but they are blind to it. Religion still has tremendous power over them. If it didn't, they wouldn't get so uptight over religious issues with people. They are still ruled by belief systems; they just changed them slightly. They think that not going to church and discontinuing other past religious activities shows that they are free from religion. Not so. Their outer physical actions may have changed, but the power of those religious mindsets and reasoning is still dwelling in them. We need an inner anarchy that goes deeper until every last stone of that crazy temple crumbles to the ground. And then we can truly dance on the ashes.

Jesus was not religious; his biggest enemies who attacked the truth he preached were the religious leaders. The same applies today. What he preached was not religious in the way we would define religion, even though he talked about his Father being God. I can talk about my earthly father and you would not say that was religious. The same applies when we talk about our "real" father—the eternal Spirit who flows through everyone. It is we who have made what Jesus said religious. We have twisted the meanings of his words to accomplish that, completely distorting the truth in the process. Jesus expected us to do this and warned us about it. He said that unless we start all over again, as little children, we can't even see the kingdom—let alone get in it! It is only when we switch to the Spirit in us—who we truly are—that we become unreligious. So the inner anarchy we need includes putting our prejudices aside and revisiting some of Jesus' words again and put them into action. That will truly free us from religion.

Jesus cannot save us or the world. He is dead. But the truth he bore witness to and demonstrated is the salvation the world is awaiting! And it's not up in the sky; it's within you and me. When we release the Spirit running through us all, we become one, and peace and love reign.

Proverbs 14:12 and 16:25 say, "There is a way that appears to be right, but in the end it leads to death." In other words, there's a form of logic or mental reasoning that makes complete sense in the way we have been taught to think by societal and religious institutions. It involves looking outside ourselves to find a reliable source for answering all the important questions about life and God. This is why people become attached to worldly, political, and religious ideologies and the people who represent them—we want to feel the security of having the "right answers." Unfortunately, there are countless ideologies out there that people debate, defend, and sometimes kill each other over. We will never resolve the questions we have by looking for answers outside ourselves. We need to shift our focus and connect our minds to another source. We need to take another look at what he said in light of our more recent understandings.

Even if you've never been personally associated with Christianity, it's likely that your view of Jesus has been tainted by how the Christian religion has characterized him and his truth. Part of the purpose of this book is to show how the typical Christian way of understanding Jesus and his teachings is simply a by-product of that same old worldly and religious reasoning.

The kind of inner anarchy we need is not swapping a traditional or conservative ideology for a more liberal or progressive one, but to stop trying to resolve things by depending on "knowledgeable" sources outside ourselves. What we need is to turn within and access the life-giving Spirit within us all. We do this by speaking out our deeper feelings and speaking honestly between us.

Yet it is much more than that. This new source of truth is not some new data that we apply like another belief system. No sir! That is where we have made a tragic mistake and stuffed everything. This is far more than some belief system in which we are expected to go around loving each other and being kind, compassionate, forgiving, non-judgmental, and accepting. While most of us admire these traits and have done our best to apply them, the results are never all that great. Let's face it: most folks have enough difficulty operating like this within a family unit, let alone across the wider universe. Instead, we want to connect with a living power. It is a power, or nature, that would allow us to live compassionately naturally . . . and a whole lot more! This power is derived from an eternal life-giving Spirit source that runs deeply through us all and is well within our reach. That is what Jesus was attempting to point us toward, demonstrating the possibility with signs and miracles.

This is what Jesus was preaching and that is why we need to take another look at his words and reinterpret them.

We have to stop pushing away what is real—the deep feelings that bubble up inside us—and trust what we experience within. We already know inside what is real and true; no one needs to tell us. Stop quoting everyone else and start speaking your truth in your own words! The source is within us. It opens up inside and shows us, but we question, doubt, and don't know what to do with it. Expressing what we feel feels silly, foolish . . . childish. But that's what it's supposed to feel like, which is why Jesus said we cannot access this dimension inside us unless we become like little children. We can help one another by speaking from these deep feelings to each other. Go on: say what you're feeling in your own words. It doesn't matter how silly it might seem. Expressing those deep feelings is always going to make you sound crazy according to the logic of the world and religion. That's ultimately what got Jesus killed.

CHAPTER FOURTEEN

Currently we are stuck in a place where the death of Jesus has no power to save anything, because the Christian religion has it trapped inside the limitations of our physical world.

IF GOD AND JESUS ARE UP IN THE SKY SOMEWHERE, THERE IS NO HOPE FOR HUMAN-KIND. WE NEED THEM HERE AND NOW.

The Christian religion's version of the salvation of the world is that the physical Jesus will someday return to earth and straighten everything out. Where is the logic in this? Jesus was already here once and the mess and misery of the world were not resolved. In fact, Jesus never said his mission was to single-handedly save the world. Instead, he said that his mission was to bear witness to and demonstrate the truth that would.

The colossal mistake of the Christian religion was building its salvation plan around the physical acts of Jesus in the world rather than what they meant in the spiritual realm—that is, in the "heavenly dimension" in us. It is an elevated state of mind. That is where we experience the reality.

But let's take a moment to discuss Christianity's version of Jesus' death. According to Christianity, the physical death of Jesus on the cross cleansed the sins of humankind, rescuing us from the wrath of God and eternal hell. Many promote this as being the "finished work of the cross"—a completed work for all time for all people. Nothing more needs to be done. Now we can all live in peace and sinless perfection. Woo hoo!

If only that were true! Seriously? Then imagine what our world would be like if sin were still running rife! Oh wait—it is. There was no sudden leap in righteousness around the globe from that day of Jesus' death twenty centuries ago, was there? Fighting among us humans didn't suddenly stop, did it? Come to think of it, the Christians were as good as any at warmongering and creating strife through the centuries.

Who is this wrathful "God" of theirs anyway, and where is the evidence that he exists? Supposedly it's the same God in times past who spoke directly to people, intervened in human affairs, and performed all kinds of miraculous acts. So what happened? Why is he not doing those things now? Why has he not shown himself to the world? Religion fights tooth and nail to defend this God. If he is as wonderful as they say, then surely he is more than capable of revealing himself?

The only rational explanation for why this God has not interjected himself miraculously into our suffering world is that this God doesn't exist. We made it all up! We have never been able to prove to the masses that this God of ours isn't dead, have we? If religion would stop defending and promoting this creature, he would simply fade away, because he is only an imaginary being in our minds. Not real at all. Not only him, but the entire system of salvation we created to appease him. That is not real either. All of this belief system is in extreme danger of crashing down, and us with it!

Does this mean that Jesus' death on the cross was meaningless? No! On the one hand, Jesus' death can be explained as simply a case of someone who threatened the religious and political powers of his day until they executed him. All this is true. And yet it's hard to miss the fact that Jesus also spoke of the significance of his death in spiritual terms. But for us to understand Jesus' teachings, we have to listen from a different place than the *cosmos* reasoning of the mind. Jesus would often allude to this when he spoke of seeing and hearing on a different level. Jesus once said, "If the eyes are good, the whole body is full of light" (Matt. 6:22). Jesus was not talking about physical eyesight; he was speaking of spiritual vision—seeing through the discernment of the Spirit. He would also often say, "Whoever has ears, let him hear" (Matt. 11:15). Jesus was not talking about physical ears and the ability to hear audible sound; he was inviting people to listen in and through the spiritual realm within them.

Jesus wanted us to understand his physical death as a demonstration of a spiritual reality. That spiritual reality reveals an understanding that shows us how we can get out of the mess of our current human condition. But for it to work, our understanding must be lifted up a level—we must see and hear with our spiritual eyes and ears.

By "spiritual," I don't mean some sort of way out there, mystical, out-of-body experience. It is very natural—it is actually the way we are designed. I refer to it as SUPERnatural only because it is accessing a different realm or source than our *cosmos* mental reasoning.

Currently we are stuck in a place where the death of Jesus has no power to save anything, because the Christian religion has it trapped inside the limitations of our physical world. In the physical realm of time and space, we have laws of science, physics, and nature that govern and regulate our reality. The crucifixion of Jesus on the cross in a world that is subject to these laws can't do anything! Magical thinking is the attribution of causal relationships between actions and events that cannot be justified by reason and observation. In this case, the magical thinking is that the bodily death of Jesus magically causes an inner cleansing and transformation. I doubt if many scientists would agree that what Jesus did on the cross two thousand years ago has taken away all their sins by cleaning up their minds. How could it?

Time and again Jesus told his disciples that it was necessary for him to die in the body, so they could then operate within the reality of his Spirit. Their attachment to Jesus the person needed to recede; it was time to stand on their own two feet. Every day that Jesus was alive in the body, he was increasingly becoming the focus of attention for his followers and detractors. Jesus, however, instructed people to find the kingdom of heaven inside themselves and to be led by the Spirit within themselves. Without Jesus' death, this transition was never going to take place. In Jesus' mind, the sooner the better. He had gathered a few followers with whom to deposit his truth, and there was nothing more for Jesus to do than demonstrate it. His remaining alive another twenty or thirty years would have prevented them from taking this crucial step of following the Spirit.

Jesus claimed that he and the "Father" were one. This has always been a difficult concept for us to get our heads around, mainly because we think of God and Jesus in physical terms. What Jesus meant by this claim is that there is only one eternal Spirit, and he was an expression of it. We too share in that same Spirit; it runs through us all. We are not separated from God because we share in the same eternal Spirit that is God, but we have been blinded to this truth. That eternal Spirit was specifically manifested in the physical Jesus who walked the land of Galilee. Why? To convey and demonstrate a solution to the problem we find ourselves in.

This is the only way our true Father-Spirit could reach us directly, because we had become spiritually deaf and blind to that Spirit within us. Two thousand years ago, our Father-Spirit became a human being like us and his name was Jesus—Emmanuel: "God with us." Several scriptures indicate that there was something unique about Jesus that separated him from others. When Jesus spoke, his words had an undeniable authority that people had not experienced before, even from their wisest rabbis. When Pilate interrogated Jesus, he found a purity of heart and spirit about Jesus that he had never encountered before and said, "I find nothing wrong in this man." And one of the most common biblical identifications for Jesus is the "lamb of God," once again pointing to this unique quality of purity, wholeness, and unity. Jesus seemed to understand this about himself and said, "I am the truth" (John 14:6).

We are told in the scriptures that Jesus represented the reality of a human being who is not corrupted by the false mentalities and ideologies that rule within the human mind. A common phrase that was used of Jesus to express this says he was "without sin." In other words, Jesus was free of the messed-up thinking that has plagued the human race. The scriptures convey this point by referring to Jesus as the "Last Adam," which implies that Jesus was demonstrating a whole new kind of human being. Once again, the Christian religion confused the truth by somehow making the physical Jesus special, when all along it was the Spirit within him. 1 Corinthians 15:45 states, "The first Adam received life, the Last Adam is a life-giving Spirit." And that is the exact same Spirit that flows through us all. What ultimately made Jesus different was the fact that his Spirit and his humanity were not divided—there was no corrupted thinking, blocking him from communicating freely with the eternal Spirit within him. This was the authority people felt in Jesus. He spoke, bore witness to, and demonstrated uncorrupted truth. This is why he came into the world!

But what did we do? We killed him and then built a great, useless religion around him on the wrong level. We made the physical Jesus into a god and overlooked that he was really explaining and demonstrating the Spirit in him—the same that is in us! That was the "God," not him! We didn't listen to what he said. Anyone who tried to understand his path was severely dealt with by the religious people who claimed to represent him. What a mess! Still today, the Christian religion focuses on the physical act of Jesus' death on the cross, so much so that the symbol of the cross has become synonymous with Christianity, and in some cases the depictions of the cross have the physical Jesus hanging on it.

But as tragic as the unjust and brutal murder of Jesus was, it created a demonstration that leads us to the truth. Jesus was aware of the significance of this, which is why he did not resist the events that ultimately led to his death. But to understand this significance, we must "see" what happened on a different level—in and through the Spirit.

Jesus himself said he was "in" this world but not "of" this world. In other words, Jesus operated within our time-space dimension that is governed by science, physics, and nature, but he was also part of a spiritual or SUPERnatural world or realm that is not limited by these laws. We are also part of that same realm! The same eternal Spirit that put Jesus there puts us there too. This is what Jesus meant when he said, "Repent (*metanoia*), for the kingdom of heaven is here." You might remember that *metanoia* means to change the way we use our minds. In other words, Jesus was saying that the SUPERnatural realm—the kingdom of heaven—is accessible to us right now, but it requires us to connect to that higher dimension within us by changing the way we use our minds. We do this by thinking in and through those deeper feelings!

Does that sound a bit too naïve and simplistic to you? If so, then you are in the right place! Jesus said unless you put your old, fixated beliefs aside and open your mind like a little child, you cannot see that dimension, let alone get in. How do you connect with and access this heavenly powerhouse within the eternal Spirit? By being a Bible scholar or following a stringent routine of meditation and other spiritual disciplines? No! We simply open our minds, put aside mental limitations, and trust those deep feelings inside us. Then express these feelings between us! There is nothing too hard about that, is there? It's just a matter of changing the way we use our minds, and then joy and freedom begin to flood us.

CHAPTER FIFTEEN

This is what saves us and the world—
the life-giving Spirit within us.

AS LONG AS WE ARE ATTACHED TO THAT PHYSICAL JESUS, CHRISTIANITY IS JUST A POWERLESS, INERT BELIEF SYSTEM—ANOTHER RELIGION BASED ON EXTERNALLY SOURCED INFORMATION FROM A HANDBOOK

It can save nothing. It blocks us from the "living" truth.

Jesus said, "Unless a kernel of wheat falls to the ground and dies, it remains only a single seed. But if it dies, it produces many seeds" (Matthew 12:24). Jesus knew that as long as the salvation of the world was tied to him personally and his actions in the world, that salvation would never come. His "going away" was a critical step that had to happen. He taught that this shift from the mortal Jesus to the immortal Spirit of Jesus within them was what would birth the power to save the world. It would cut down the ruling mindsets within us that are destroying us and lift up a higher living presence and dimension that would unite us. Jesus said, "And when I am lifted up from the earth, I will draw everyone to myself" (John 12:32). This was not a challenge for people to start a Jesus religion and go around the world trying to convert people to it. Jesus was saying that when the eternal Spirit—within him and us—is lifted up out of us into the world, then that eternal Spirit will be easily recognizable to us all and draw us together as one human family.

We have all been made aware of the distinction that Jesus is the "lamb of God that takes away the sin of the world." In fact, one scripture states this as "the lamb slain from the foundation of the world" (Rev. 13:8). The verse is followed by that little instruction for us to heed: "If any man have an ear, let him hear" (Rev. 13:9). In other words, to understand the meaning of this, it requires hearing in those deep feelings of the Spirit.

The foundation of the world was long before the mortal Jesus arrived on the scene. Jesus stated to the religious leaders who were arguing about being descendants of Abraham, that "before Abraham, I was" (John 8:58). There are no scriptural reports documenting that the physical Jesus was wandering around on earth back then, are there? This makes it clear that we are dealing with two different realms. This is where the Christian religion has confused the life, truth, and teachings of Jesus. They are thinking of Jesus on the wrong level. Jesus offered water to the Samaritan woman at the well. She took Jesus' words to mean that he was literally offering her a supply of drinking water. But Jesus clarified that he was offering "living water."

This confusion applies to Jesus' death. There are actually two different dimensions in which Jesus' crucifixion took place that represent two separate levels. The physical crucifixion of Jesus on the cross in our space and time dimension did not accomplish anything. How could it? That's the magical thinking the Christian religion has been dragging around for two thousand years. And where has it gotten us?! The physical crucifixion of Jesus was pointing to a timeless truth within the spiritual dimension, namely that the eternal Spirit is within us. This is what saves us and the world—the life-giving Spirit within us. What kind of "life" does that Spirit give? That life is eternal life, God life, heaven life, abundant life, protected life, whole life. Jesus bore witness to and demonstrated that life, and he had to die so we would understand that this was not fundamentally "his" life but "our" life—a fact established "from the foundation of the world."

So why did Jesus have to die? Jesus had to die because our eternal Father-Spirit wanted to wake us up to this reality: there is nothing and no one in this world that can save us. The only thing that has this power is the Spirit within us. Until we let all our human reasoning, all our worldly and religious attachments and dependencies, and all our cosmos mindsets and ideologies die, we are stuck. It is only the eternal Jesus that can save us, which is that eternal Spirit within us.

The most popular scripture of the Christian religion is John 3:16, which says, "For God so loved the world that he sent his only begotten son that whosoever trusts in him shall live on forever." What we haven't realized is that this "son"—the eternal Spirit—has been sent and has been in us since the beginning!

Not only did Jesus highlight this truth to us through his brutal slaying on the cross, he also demonstrated the power from this timeless transaction that was already in him by doing miracles, healings, deliverances, and speaking truth. He said we could do the same—even greater works than he did! Sadly, Christians have made the fatal mistake of crediting these experiences as coming from their Sky God in heaven up in the clouds somewhere.

Christianity's false understanding of the death of Jesus means there are only two ways of reaching the "heavenly dimension"—either by dying and being taken up to God or by Jesus bringing it down with him when he returns. Meanwhile, Jesus taught and demonstrated that this dimension—the heavenly powerhouse—is present right now within us! The whole box of tricks! For the past two thousand years, Christians should have been the ones opening that box. Instead, we've had it cemented shut!

The scriptures say that our Father-Spirit only ever created "one son" with the purpose of bringing us all back home together in that same nature that runs through all of us. Jesus said, "No one comes to the Father except by me" (John 14:6). In other words, it is not necessary to divide up the world and people in thousands of different religions, all arguing about who has the correct theology. All that is necessary is for all of us to turn to that eternal Spirit that is within us. As Jesus said, "I in them and you in me, that they may be perfected into a unit, so that the world may know that you sent me, and loved them, even as you have loved me" (John 17:23). We can't get much closer than that.

There are growing signs that this love and togetherness is now seeping into our world. People are reaching out toward one another in a deeper and more honest way as the hold of religion begins to weaken. Jesus said, "Truly I tell you, this generation will certainly not pass away until all these things have happened. Heaven and earth will pass away, but my words will never pass away" (Matt. 24:35).

Jesus knew he was called to testify to the truth, and that even his death was necessary so humankind would understand that we needed to inherit his Spirit for ourselves. Though the reality of the eternal Spirit within us was a fact established before the foundation of the world, the death of Jesus awakens us to the need to claim it for ourselves. He died to the cosmos to pass over his Spirit to us. All that nature was passed over and is embedded in the depths of each of us, and is ready to be lifted up in and out of us.

If this reality was true before the foundation of the world, then why has the world continued down this path of suffering and destruction? Here's why: there are 7 billion people on the planet—2.5 billion of them are Christians who have corrupted the truth of Jesus for themselves and, in the process, have alienated the other 4.5 billion people from even considering it! What all 7 billion of us need to do is stop thinking about Jesus as a religion and instead embrace his truth, which is to let our worldly selves die—namely, the false mindsets and ideologies ruling and destroying us from within—and rise up in that nature, Spirit, and life that we all share as our common spiritual inheritance.

Two things must take place for this to happen. First, we have to kill off the Sky God we've created. Let this "God" and this "Jesus" die, and let your entire cosmos ways of reasoning die with them. This is the inner anarchy we need! We must tear down every stone of that worldly and religious "temple" until there isn't one left standing. Each of us must become an atheist to that worldly and religious "God" and the systems attached to them. We cannot embrace the truth that Jesus taught and demonstrated and keep that false God and system alive. It has to come down!

If we keep believing that this Sky God still exists, then we are still ruled by our corrupt minds, waiting for some future day when we are magically beamed up into some heaven beyond the clouds. We can't get out of this until we let all of this die, and we bury it with Jesus in his grave.

The second thing we must do is officially take possession of the nature, Spirit, and life that Jesus said was willed over to us before the foundation of the world. That is the true resurrection and return of Jesus we've been waiting for—for the eternal Spirit to be lifted up within and out of us into this world. That is when that heavenly powerhouse is opened up and we birth a new order, making life "on earth as it is in heaven."

What this means is that we don't have to die to access the dimension that saves the world and brings us into heaven. It is all already done within us! Pretty good deal, isn't it?!

Now what? Accept the deal! Acknowledge that Jesus the person is dead and take up the legacy of the eternal Spirit within you. Unless we take this step, we are going to be wandering around in circles for another two thousand years and getting nowhere. You can't have it both ways—keeping Jesus alive and taking up his Spirit. Keeping Jesus alive keeps us attached to a lie and a corrupt system of thinking that is blocking the way. We must put Jesus back in that grave. It was never about Jesus the person; it was always about the eternal Spirit that was within Jesus and is within us. We need to stop worshipping the person Jesus and start living within the reality of the eternal Spirit!

Jesus bore witness to and demonstrated the reality of God and humankind functioning as one unit, bound together by the same eternal Spirit. The extraordinary life that Jesus lived was a result of connecting with and operating in and through the dimension of that Spirit. Jesus' closest followers became enamored with Jesus himself, which eventually became their biggest obstacle for embracing and living from that Spirit. Two thousand years later, Christians are still worshipping Jesus the person, but are not laying hold of his Spirit within them. Further, the Christian religion has distracted the world with this Jesus-worship and failed to deliver the truth that Jesus taught. Jesus' knew that his death was central to his message. As long as people attached the divine of the Spirit to him personally, they would not be able to truly grasp that each of them were as one with God—connected by that same eternal Spirit—as he was.

We cannot get full access to this life while we believe that the Godhead, or whatever we wish to call it, still lives beyond ourselves. As already mentioned, practically speaking, that puts us in a state of unbelief. And to make matters worse, we Christians are the ones who have been ordained to make it all happen, and because we haven't got it right, we have blocked the way for everyone and ourselves! We actually teach the world our unbelief!

It is just as mad as people asking Jesus into their hearts and then spending the rest of their lives looking for him up in the sky! We become double- minded: he's here in my heart; no, he's up in the blue yonder. See how our minds keep deceiving us and stop us from making a firm decision?

Jesus painted a spiritual picture of what happens when we turn toward the truth—our old, corrupted, screwed-up soul life is "crucified" with him. He takes it into oblivion as that "lamb that is slain." We are cleansed from our unbelief—its power over us has been broken! He passes his life to us and we live on . . . forever. It is a free gift, all done inside us, in the blink of an eye, and we can have it now.

Start rebelling! Switch your allegiance. That starts birthing the real "savior" into our world. As Isaiah 9:6-7 says,

For a child has been born—for us!
    the gift of a son—for us!
He'll take over
    the running of the world.
His names will be: Amazing Counselor,
    Strong God,
Eternal Father,
    Prince of Wholeness.
His ruling authority will grow,
    and there'll be no limits to the wholeness he brings.

That "child" is the eternal Spirit within each of us. Rather than submit to those corrupt mindsets and ideologies ruling the world, let's tear those down and instead lift out that "Strong God" and "Prince of Wholeness" that is alive in each of us. That's who should be running this world!

CHAPTER SIXTEEN

*As boldly as the Christian church has preached
their view of heaven, you would think you'd find
plenty of evidence that Jesus supported it.*

HEAVEN IS THE ACE IN THE HOLE OF THE CHRISTIAN RELIGION.

It's the trump card. The promise of heaven is the hope that keeps Christians believing. No matter the hardships that befall their lives or the suffering they see in the world, believers derive a sense of comfort and justice from the idea that there will be a huge payoff in the end. Heaven is regarded as where things finally happen—where Christians' hopes, rewards, and bliss will materialize. Heaven is the place where salvation is fulfilled and the good life begins—where all the believers are having a ball in their white nightgowns, walking up and down streets of gold and worshipping their God in glory. They have arrived!

Some things about this heaven just don't add up. How can the "good news" be that we must endure a lifetime of difficulty, misery, and suffering only to get sick and die a miserable death so we can finally be happy and fulfilled? If you went to a restaurant that advertised exquisite cuisine, but said you had to first eat all the rotten food out of the back dumpster to get the good stuff, would you? I'm guessing not! Surely many people reach the end of their life and look back and wonder what the purpose of it was—especially as they leave all their grieving loved ones behind. That is cruel.

And there is something else that doesn't add up about the Christian religion's ideas of heaven. Up until now, no one has been there and come back and been able to authentically verify those ideas. While it is true that people have had near-death experiences and spoken of very real spiritual and mystical experiences, there is no scientific hard evidence that proves that heaven exists somewhere out there. It is still very much a theory that Christians cling to. If we were so certain that this belief of heaven as a perfect paradise is so infallible, then why not put a bullet in our heads and go there now?! Woo hoo! We are out of here! Christians should be racing each other to see who can get there first!

But, despite all the misery of the world, most of us don't want to die. Instead, we do everything we can to slow down, hold off, and prevent death. We fight tooth and nail to cling to life for as long as we can here on earth—Christians as much as anyone. We spend billions and billions on medical research, doctors, and hospitals. Dying is the last activity we want to take part in.

As boldly as the Christian church has preached their view of heaven, you would think you'd find plenty of evidence that Jesus supported it. But Jesus painted quite a different picture.

The Christian religion locates God, Jesus, and heaven up in the sky. But let's be honest here: what power have you ever truly experienced coming down from the sky . . . other than perhaps a tornado? On the other hand, if heaven—the nucleus of divine power—is not up in the sky, then where is it? Where is that source of eternal life, energy, power, vitality, and happiness?

If you really pondered it, I think you'd find that the truly deep and powerful experiences you've had in life happened within you or came out of you. Though something externally might trigger them, those powerful feelings are a reality that flows and emanates from within you. You might be hiking a scenic trail along a river and suddenly experience deep feelings of peace and well-being well up from within you. Or perhaps a full feeling of love bubbles up inside you, and you express it in caring, kindness, or compassion. We tend to focus on the environment in these scenarios (being outdoors) or the action (the expression of kindness), but overlook the fact that the nucleus of these powerful and satisfying deep feelings are happening from within us. If we are truly honest, we have encountered, at odd times, some very real, joyful love sensations from a source deep within us. That should be a clue to where the source is—not out there/up there somewhere, but inside us!

That's some solid evidence of where that powerhouse is located. And these deep inner feelings can happen with anyone, regardless of a person's belief system. Of course, Christians adamantly claim those feelings would be impossible if you were not a serious, Christian, God-believing person to start with. And even so, they would say, we should never trust our feelings—that could be the devil misleading us! Instead, we should always reference our Bibles for guidance. To Christians, the Bible has the final word. It is their God.

CHAPTER SEVENTEEN

*Feel that life, Spirit, and nature within you.
It has the authority to birth a whole new world!*

BUT WITH SO MUCH DEPENDENCE UPON THE BIBLE—THAT MAGIC BOOK—ONE WON-
DERS JUST HOW WELL THEY READ IT THEMSELVES?

It creates a lot of division. Jesus said that the goal was for all of us to be united in one spiritual life. He said, "For all of them to become one heart and mind. Just as you, Father, are in me and I in you, so they might be one heart and mind with us" (John 17:21). How can that oneness be possible if that spiritual life is in God and Jesus (who are located in heaven somewhere up there in the sky) or in a book? Oneness is only possible because that life and Spirit were given to us! Jesus made it quite clear. He said we will dwell in them and they in us. This "we" and "us" is the fullness of the life of God—that's the powerhouse! That life and power were willed over to us and are in us. Jesus even told his disciples that his Father would make his abode within us!

Have we been seriously overlooking some very basic logic? Jesus preached that the kingdom of heaven was within our reach. No more than an arm's length away. That was his central message! And, as already stated, there is some pretty convincing experiential evidence of deep stuff going on in us at times—far more than anyone has noticed coming from out of the sky. Shouldn't we be taking a look at that?

Christians claim that God's power is in heaven (located up in the sky), where they will all go into their wonderful life of eternal state of spiritual blessedness. But if this is the case, that powerhouse in the sky needs some new batteries, because it has made very little difference here on earth. And if there is such a place above, populated with those who have passed on, why haven't at least a few of them revealed themselves and their heavenly experience to erase all doubt?

It seems strange that all these people up there haven't been agitated enough to get their God or Jesus to do something about their poor fellow brethren stuck down here having a hard time. The atrocities that have been going on down here over the centuries are diabolical. If heaven is God's headquarters and the nucleus of his saving power, then why haven't they done this for us? They are letting us down badly. For two thousand years, many of us valiantly preaching his name have had one hell of a hard time. Why is it that the God of heaven has not answered our calls for help?

The answer seems simple. If there is not a God or Jesus located up in the sky somewhere, then it follows that there can't be some heaven up there either.

Once you tear down that carnal mental reasoning that externalizes and materializes God, Jesus, and heaven into physical people and places out there somewhere, then you can see the truth to which Jesus bore witness. If we take another look at things with the assumption that heaven and what it represents are located in us, and not in the sky, the old, traditional Christian beliefs get turned inside out and look plainly ridiculous.

One place you can see it is in the "Lord's Prayer." Jesus prayed, "Our Father, who is in heaven, hallowed be your name. Your kingdom come, on earth as it is in heaven."

Christians imitate that prayer as follows: with heads bowed and thoughts and words projected up to the sky, they say, "Our Sky God, located out there in a place called heaven, we worship you in all your power and glory. May the kingdom that you established up there in heaven be what you bring down and institute here on earth." They understand it very much in "physical" terms. But what good does that do for anyone? They have been intoning that for hundreds of years! I have done it myself more times than I can count.

But if you lift up Jesus' words a level, you see a different scenario. This "Father" is that higher spiritual presence—his nature and authority—that Jesus said was within us. His life and Spirit were willed over to us. That "heaven" is an elevated dimension of power, eternity, and happiness—it's a sensation or reality that manifests within us. "Hallowed be your name" is an acknowledgment of that new Spirit or mind nature within us. The "kingdom" is authority, and it is all set to go to be manifested "on earth as it is in heaven." Those heavenly feelings within us are finally allowed to express themselves on earth. We speak them . . . and all becomes renewed!

If you were to write out the Lord's Prayer from that higher understanding, it would say, "Turn toward that higher spiritual presence within you that operates in an elevated dimension of power and happiness inside you. Feel that life, Spirit, and nature within you. It has the authority to birth a whole new world! Express those heavenly feelings within you—speak them, and all will be made new."

Could it be that simple? I think so. We should help each other to give it a go. Why not? What have we got to lose? Only this crappy life we have now.

This is the salvation Jesus promised in John 3:16.

For God (that higher spiritual presence and source of life and power)

so loved the world (our world in captivity to the powers of those mind sets that rule within us)

that he gave his only begotten son (became one of us to bear witness to and demonstrate the truth)

that whoever believes in him (trusts and clings to the truth)
shall not perish (not taste death)
but have eternal life (but have whole, secure, abundant, continuing life forever)

That "only begotten son," which literally means "one of a unique kind," has always been sent to straighten out our world and save us. Not from up in the sky, but within us. We have been carrying that "one of unique kind" around within us for centuries and haven't realized it—a little detail the Christian experts never told us.

CHAPTER EIGHTEEN

We are the ones to close the door on this age
of suffering and death and birth a new world
of abundance and life eternal!

JESUS SAID TO HER, "I AM THE RESURRECTION AND THE LIFE; HE WHO BELIEVES IN ME WILL LIVE EVEN IF HE DIES. AND EVERYONE WHO LIVES AND BELIEVES IN ME WILL NEVER DIE. DO YOU BELIEVE THIS?" (JOHN 11:25-26).

These are two statements that Jesus made. The first declaration is "I am the resurrection and the life; he who believes in me will live even if he dies." Christians would have no problem agreeing with that. Perhaps they would add a few conditions from their particular denomination's teachings, but that's the guts of it for them. That is pretty much their gospel. That gets a thumbs up. "Yep! We believe in Jesus so we earn a one-way trip to heaven after we die."

But what about the second statement? "Everyone who lives and believes in me *will never die*" is followed by his rather pointed question, "Do you believe this?"

Is it just me, or does it sound like Jesus is actually saying that it is not necessary for people to die? It's a bit difficult to gloss over these words, especially since after saying them, he asks this direct and penetrating question, testing the willingness to believe, trust, and accept his claim. This isn't the only place where Jesus makes this jaw-dropping claim. In John 8:51, he says: "I assure you, most solemnly I tell you, if anyone observes my teaching he will by no means ever see and experience death." In the next verse we are told that Jesus' assertion was so distressing to the religious leaders that one of them responded by saying, "Now we know that you are under the power of a demon" (John 8:52). This guy was from among a group of Jews who are recorded as believing Jesus (like many around today), but even they were upset. "Abraham died, and the prophets too. Who do you make yourself to be?" (John 8:53).

This message of not having to go through death that Jesus preached was obviously a real issue. When he was carrying on about being the bread of life that had come down from heaven, and if they ate of him they would live on forever without dying really got them uptight. He told them, "Your fathers ate the manna in the wilderness and died. I am the true bread, eat of me and you'll not die at all! It is the Spirit that gives life, your flesh profits nothing" (John 6:49,51,63).

This was just getting too much for some of his followers. "As a result of this many of His disciples withdrew and were not walking with Him anymore" (John 6:66).

I can't ever remember hearing a sermon about people never dying, and I know for sure I never preached one in all my years as a Christian pastor. Most Christians would say, "No way! We can't take these words literally. Jesus could not have meant that people would never die. That's way over the top. The Christian church has never taught about people not dying. It is ordained that man should die." Yet there it is, printed in black and white in their beloved Bibles.

What then shall we believe?

Evangelical Christians regularly use the word "saved." A major thrust of their ministry is to "save" people. Hours of planning and scheming go into how to win more souls. Countless people have been confronted with the question "Are you saved?" This is usually followed by a few threats about what will happen to you if you are not!

The Greek word for "save" (*sozo*) that Jesus used when talking about saving the world is quite an all-encompassing word. It means "to save;

to keep safe and sound; to rescue from danger or destruction; to deliver or protect; to heal and preserve; to be made whole; and to be abundantly supplied." It has nothing to do with asking Jesus into your heart, going to church, Bible study, doing good works, and then getting sick and dying with the hope that you are going to make it to heaven. That scenario hardly fits the definition or scope of that word.

Jesus said, "He that endures (abides) to the end shall be saved" (Matt. 24:13). This implies that if we can hang in there, we will eventually come into the full realization of all that the word "saved" means.

But how could this work? It seems a bit far-fetched that this could mean that we don't die. Last I checked, everyone dies. This is certainly one of those mindsets that have ruled within us that no one would think to question. But consider how much pain, suffering, heartache, brokenness, and despair are associated with the experience of death. It's a dark cloud that is continually and ominously hanging over all our heads. Does this line up with the kind of salvation Jesus promised to the world—to be delivered, protected, healed, made whole, abundantly supplied, and preserved? It doesn't! We have always accepted that death is just part of the deal. But what if Jesus was offering a different deal?

Is there something that would have to take place in our world for this reality to be realized?

Although it is generally overlooked, the main message Jesus preached was about his expected return and the implications of it. Jesus described a scenario in which our world would be falling apart at the seams, saying this would be a sign of the end of an age. The Gospel of Luke describes a complete unraveling of the social fabric with widespread calamity and war. As frightening as these descriptions are, I'd have to say that they sound uncomfortably similar to what I read in the headlines each day. Jesus told many parables to warn us about the end of an age, telling us to be vigilant, continually on the alert, prepared, and aware that his return could swiftly unfold without warning. He also said that his return would coincide with the world being under terrific stress and difficulty and with humankind in desperate need of rescuing.

Sounds awfully close to our present situation, doesn't it? We are fast reaching the point of our world problems being beyond the reasoning and efforts of mortal human beings. We keep doing all we can and yet our planet and society are breaking down everywhere. We desperately need a real savior! We need access to a superior mind and authority.

Fundamentalists and evangelicals are very good at painting this apocalyptic picture of total collapse and a horrendous bloodbath on earth and then being rescued by a "physical" Jesus with blazing eyes, waving a sword and plummeting out of the skies. They have scared the hell out of many people with this "Left Behind" story in which born-again Christians are snatched up from earth into heaven, leaving the rest of humankind behind to either comply with the evil regime of the antichrist or refuse and be starved, raped, tortured, and beheaded. These preachers feel quite assured of their story of doom and gloom. They are confident they have done the right thing; it's those suckers out there who are going to suffer, they think. They say with their self-righteous attitude, "They should have listened to us. We warned them so. The end is near, and it's all going to come crashing down on their heads. When our Jesus comes back, that is the end of the world. They will be swept up in the fury of God's wrath, and we will be beamed up to streets of gold."

There is the end of an age that is coming, but it's not going to look like that. The principles apply, but the boot will be on the other foot. They thought they were first, but they will be last—the ones who, as Jesus said, did not have the ears to hear his truth.

Jesus said that when he returns, it will not be the physical Jesus dropping down from the sky, but his "presence" that manifests here on earth. This "presence" is lifted up and out of us into the world. It's the powerhouse dimension that rescues us from a world that is collapsing under the weight of our powerless ideas and failed reasoning. Jesus said about this reality that "the powers of the heavens will be shaken" because of it. That higher spiritual presence and eternal dimension will open up from within us, shine into our world, and challenge beliefs we thought would last forever. The old age of human mortality will pass away, and the new messianic age will begin. In fact, the phrase Jesus used in John 8:51 for not dying, or not going through death, translated literally means "to live on to the messianic age."

Jesus said, "Truly, truly, if anyone keeps my word, death by no means will he behold unto the messianic age" (John 8:51).

Jesus gave his life to give birth to that new age. It can never happen with him up in the clouds on the throne of the Christian religion. In John 14:6 Jesus said, "I am the truth." What truth is that? God and humankind, not separated by time or space, but one. We have yet to truly embrace and manifest that truth. When we do, that oneness will spill over into what Jesus described as "on earth as it is in heaven." It's hard to imagine, isn't it? Heaven on earth? People not dying? And yet Jesus pointed to the unfolding of a reality that would surpass what he experienced, and said we would do "greater things."

What could those greater things be? Could it be overcoming death?

In John 11 is a well-known passage about the death of Lazarus. Jesus discussed the condition of Lazarus with his disciples. He told them that Lazarus was asleep, and he was going to awaken him. The disciples responded that sleep was good, because it would help him get well (verse 12). Jesus then plainly told them that "Lazarus is dead" (verse 14). Notice that Jesus stated emphatically that Lazarus was dead, but at the same time that he described death as a condition like sleep. When the time came for Jesus to act, "He cried with a loud voice, 'Lazarus, come forth!' And he who had died came out bound by hand and foot with graveclothes . . . Jesus said to them, 'Loose him, and let him go'" (versus 43,44). Lazarus had not gone to heaven or hell. He had been entombed, where he "slept" in death until Jesus called him out of the grave by resurrection.

Christians have been told that people who are in their graves now will be resurrected, rising to meet the messiah returning in the sky. But if the Spirit of Jesus and the authority of the kingdom of heaven is within us, wouldn't we now be the ones awakening the dead from their sleep? If we truly take the message of Jesus to heart, the reality is that for those who are presently alive and those who have died, full salvation is engineered by us living on this side of death. Christians have it backward, waiting for some God out there to figure it all out in the end. The reality is that God is within us here and now, and there's nothing to wait for.

Jesus is neither a demon, as the religious leaders claimed, nor is he the "savior" as the Christian religion has taught. Jesus left this world in body because he knew he would return in spirit, and this is the salvation of the world we have been waiting for. We are the spiritual body of Christ! We are the spiritual Bethlehem! We are the heavenly powerhouse with the authority to save ourselves and the world! We are the household and family that brings forth the living bread that operates within a dimension that is not limited to the laws of science, physics, and nature! We are the ones to close the door on this age of suffering and death and birth a new world of abundance and life eternal!

Jesus asked, "Do you believe this?" Will you believe this?

You already know all of this is true. You have been on that road to Emmaus, and you have felt that burning in your heart—that voice, that presence, those deep feelings within you. Emmaus means a "warm, flowing stream." Watching a sunset, listening to a score of music, holding your lover's hand, feeling a sense of oneness with all in your heart—I know you have felt this! That is what's real and true! It's what those deep feelings were pointing you toward and showing you. You know that it doesn't make any sense for our world to continue suffering. There is no theological explanation that is ever going to make any of this okay. Jesus spoke this truth and gave his life for it. The "Father" came into this world in Jesus to save us. To shows us the way. To bear witness to the truth and demonstrate it on a level we could understand. You cannot turn back. We are the "return of Christ." We are here to bring our current age to an end and open a new messianic age. We don't need gurus and scholars; we need people to become like children and listen to that voice within them . . . and then speak it.

Now is the day of salvation!

"Go to the lost sheep of the house of Israel (the Jesus believers). And as you go, preach, saying, 'The kingdom of heaven is at hand.' Heal the sick, raise the dead, cleanse the lepers, cast out demons. Freely you received, freely give" (Matt. 10:6-8).

CHAPTER NINETEEN

*Metanoia is a condition for birthing the kingdom of heaven
into our world, because it is turning to and speaking
from that deeper source where the true power is.*

IT'S TIME FOR ME TO TURN THIS OVER TO YOU.

We are now at that point in the journey where my contribution is done, and it's up to you to take it from here. It's not easy for me to say this. This is my fifth book, and over the years I have acquired the reputation of being a well-known spiritual teacher, mentor, and author. I have more social media "friends," "followers," and "fans" than I can count and was recently dubbed as "one of the great spiritual voices of our times." Pretty impressive for a guy who still types with two fingers and dreams of qualifying for the Tour de France.

I know it's time for me to step aside, but there's a way I've been fighting it tooth and nail, which became especially evident to me in writing this chapter.

As I write this book, I send rough drafts of chapters to a few ex-Institutional-Christian friends for input and feedback. That was humbling! A few of them were like, "Seriously, Jim; we're back to quoting Bible verses?!" That didn't go over too well! It wasn't easy convincing them that this was not just a rehash of their old religion. Having just spent years shedding religion, they were fearful of getting sucked right back into it. Maybe others of you felt the same.

Hopefully I succeeded in persuading them that what this book is about is nothing like that. But to lift up what is real and shine the light on where all this is going, it was necessary to untangle the mess the Christian religion had made of Jesus and his teachings. It was critical to see that Jesus taught that the God and heaven we have all been waiting for up in the sky have been in us all along. Once we get that, we can let that entire mindset and system die off and become obsolete.

After cautiously putting that fear aside and continuing on, the next major concern that arose had to do with a more practical matter. Although people could see that we were heading toward something pretty amazing and exciting, they wanted to know exactly what they had to do to make it work. If I heard it once, I heard it a hundred times. "Okay, Jim, that all sounds well and good, but how do we make all this happen? What do we do?"

And that's when Guru Jim—"one of the great spiritual voices of our times"—jumped into action. Help was on its way! That's what this chapter was going to be—Jim Palmer handing over the secret formula and new program for throwing this thing out into the world. This chapter was meant to be the troubleshooting guide for this new way and the definitive explanation on how to implement it all step-by-step. Yep, I planned on chapter 19 singlehandedly answering any feasible question about what to do. This was meant to be the DIY instructions for birthing a new world . . . for dummies.

Wow! What I learned in attempting to write such a chapter is that the only dummy around here was me . . . aka "one of the great spiritual boneheads of our times."

Tell people what to do? Seriously? How do you tell people what to do when we are talking about a world that will completely displace what we are living in now? And how do you explain the nuts and bolts of moving toward this higher eternal dimension in which it's not even necessary to go through a normal death to get there? Think about it. It will no longer be necessary for priests to offer last rites or Christian pastors to lead funerals, and we will most definitely need a major career transition assistance plan for all those funeral home directors and morticians. But it even goes further than that! Jesus said we will do far greater works than he did. What is that going to look like?

I'm not sure what advice I can give. I'm way out of my league with this one. I'm pretty much in the same boat we all are, sailing into uncharted territory. What would it mean to have heaven on earth? I'm not sure even J.R.R. Tolkien's imagination can stretch that far.

I do know this much, though—this is the reality and possibility to which Jesus pointed. Once you disentangle Jesus from Christianity to see this, you basically have only two options: option A—Jesus was crazy and we just need to move on with our lives as they are—or option B— maybe what Jesus was saying warrants further investigation. When I listened to those deep feelings within me, I was drawn to option B. You're going to have to turn inside and decide this for yourself.

So here we are on the brink of exploring a whole new frontier without really having the foggiest idea how this is going to open up. I can't tell you exactly how all this is going to play out, but I have a few suspicions.

Jesus was a physical demonstration and expression of the eternal life-giving Spirit, and so one indication of what this might look like is Jesus himself. Don't think of this in terms of the Christian religion's obsession with the WWJD (What Would Jesus Do) question, which puts the focus on the physical Jesus and his external actions, deeds, and behaviors. Rather than asking what Jesus would do, a better question would be "How did Jesus do it?" Jesus knew and spoke truth with authority. He was operating within a whole different dimension that was beyond our time-space limitations and the laws of science and nature. What's critical to understand is that you have access to that same eternal life-giving Spirit that powered Jesus. The words and actions of Jesus were originating from the same source. That same authority from which Jesus spoke and acted is in us. That is who we listen to. That is our true teacher. That is the heavenly powerhouse from which we speak, live, love, and set each other free.

The common-sense observation is that for this to work, we are going to have to turn toward, listen to, follow, and walk in tune with that source. This is exactly what Jesus meant when he called for "repentance" (*metanoia*) and to "follow me"—to switch to that deeper mind within us (the Spirit) and follow that. We are going to help each other make contact with that. It's not going to be easy, because most of us learned through religion that we are bad at our cores and can't trust anything inside us.

But if we switch to that deeper mind within us, the prospect of birthing a new reality "on earth as it is in heaven" is a real possibility. In fact, it's a certainty!

Jesus once described what this reality would look like. He said, "In that day you will not question Me about anything. Truly, truly, I say to you, if you ask the Father for anything in My name, He will give it to you" (John 16:23). This particular translation makes the point well by capitalizing the pronouns referring to Jesus, because he is not speaking of himself, but the Spirit within him—the same eternal Spirit that is the "Father," and the same eternal Spirit that is within each of us. That Spirit of love is the source, power, and authority to deliver the kind of "salvation" Jesus described—healing, wholeness, abundance, protection, well-being, and in the end, continuous living.

Jesus told his disciples, "Until now you have asked me for nothing *in my name (my nature!)*, ask and I will do it for you" (John 16:24). How is that for a deal? But once again, we must connect with the Spirit within us and NOT with an imaginary "physical" Jesus out there. Only then will we see things happen. We are going to have to help each other to make that connection. Did I already say that? I can't say it enough. We are not going to get anywhere unless we help each other connect with that source within us.

Isn't it ridiculous when you consider that there have been two thousand years of Christian prayers that have not delivered the kind of salvation Jesus described? There has been a huge amount of scholarly writings devoted to the study of prayer, and yet they haven't seen the obvious. It is a wonder why someone didn't tap scholars on the shoulder and draw their attention to the fact that it doesn't work that way. The word "prayer" literally means a "projected wish." Its real substance and power is when we speak it from that true source. It cannot be done like the Pharisees by intoning repetitious stuff from our heads. That is how we were trained, but it will never work. This is why *metanoia* is a condition for birthing the kingdom of heaven into our world, because it is turning to and speaking from that deeper source where the true power is. This is what Jesus meant when he said, "Ask anything in my name." He was not teaching a magic formula, whereby divine power is somehow mysteriously released through the physical utterance of his name. Jesus was saying that when we project a wish or desire in, through, and from that higher spirit presence within us, it carries the power and authority to manifest it. I'm stuck here as a writer between needing to represent the full import of what Jesus taught, while knowing it will be tempting to create another magic formula out of it. Jesus taught that the best way to embrace his truth was to come at it as a child.

Jesus demonstrated this reality himself in those actions we call "miraculous." Once again, religion led us astray by telling us that only Jesus could do these things because he was special. But this is not what Jesus himself said. Jesus said we would do even greater works than he did. Still others will say that this sort of elevated or higher living won't happen until some future day in heaven. And yet, these miraculous acts of Jesus happened in the world as it was. Jesus never raised people's expectations about some future paradise. Instead, his message was that the kingdom of heaven is here now, not somewhere else and later.

Jesus once said, "Without me you can do nothing" (John 15:5). That does not mean we have to somehow track down that Jesus, who is dead anyway, before things can happen—like Christians have been trying to do for centuries. No, it means that without connecting with that Spirit of love and life within us, we can do nothing. Continuing on, Jesus said, "Your flesh profits nothing" (John 6:63). The "flesh" here refers to our natural being—how we normally live in this world. That way won't work.

Here is a fuller definition of the "flesh" for those who want to get the full impact of this: the body, as opposed to the spirit, or as the symbol of what is external; human nature with its frailties and limitations; a human being—carnal-minded, fleshly, crude, and earthbound.

We can't do miracles by using our natural minds. That's why we don't see them.

Jesus would have never healed anyone apart from triggering the life-giving Spirit within people. That's why he said, whenever someone was healed, that the power that caused it was released from within them, "Your faith has made you whole!" We are also told that in one region Jesus couldn't trigger these miracles because of their lack of trust, "He did not do any mighty works because of their unbelief" (Matt. 13:58). The Spirit was locked up within them. That pretty much describes our situation for the past twenty centuries, doesn't it? Largely because of how the Christian religion has mishandled the truth of Jesus.

CHAPTER TWENTY

One of the biggest threats to birthing this new reality
will be the temptation to create a new religion out of it.

THIS LIFE AND VITALITY DID BEGIN TO BREAK OUT IN THE '60S WHEN MANY OF THE YOUNGER ENLIGHTENED FOLK BEGAN TO QUESTION THE ACCEPTED THINKING AND BEHAVIOR OF THE RULING ESTABLISHMENT.

Helped along by their music, the hippie culture gained an awareness of their feelings that was growing and revealing a higher dimension—a dimension that no one was around to explain to them. No one knew at the time. They were just at the point of identifying the source when the Christians moved in and managed to hijack the natural and spontaneous outpouring by adding its religious thinking, structures, and programs. It was soon turned into the spectacle and farce of the charismatic movement.

However, many of those folks still around (older and wiser) probably look back to those days of love, peace, and joy with nostalgia. Consider this a personal invitation to do a bit of inner anarchy, challenge the system, and start showing the way!

I shouldn't be too critical of how the Christian religion killed off the Spirit at work in the '60s, because I was flirting with the possibility of doing a similar thing in this book. After the demand died down for writing a chapter giving people directions, I managed to take on another harebrained idea. I figured that the least I could do was outline a set of principles we could all adopt and follow. Yes, that was the ticket! I was set on writing an Inner Anarchy Manifesto. I could just envision it being shared all over Facebook and Tweeted to the masses!

That would have been a colossal mistake, taking us down the same old path as before.

But the more I thought about it, I realized that this is not your normal belief system. Actually, it's not a belief system at all. This is a living Spirit energy power source . . . thing. This can't be reduced to some set of beliefs, however cleverly I might be able to explain them. This Spirit power source is an entity in its own right, and is far greater than anything my pea brain could ever come up with. It's that Spirit source itself that is the only true authority capable of providing the answers we need. Hmm. Rather than trying to drag it down into our limited mental reasoning, maybe we should just open ourselves fully and listen to that. The last thing I want to do is try to usurp that ultimate dominion of power or stand in its way by trying to be "one of the great spiritual voices of our times." All I really need to do is encourage people to plug in themselves and listen to it. Maybe that at least will make me "one of the great people connectors to the Spirit." Oh, never mind.

One of the biggest threats to birthing this new reality will be the temptation to create a new religion out of it. This is just what humans do when we are left to our worldly *cosmos* reasoning. We can't help doing this when we are operating in that dimension. That is how we are trained. Many of these folk are well meaning with good intentions. But we are just like the Israelites who, instead of dealing directly with God, demanded a king to rule over them to be like other nations. Likewise, rather than going directly to the source within each of us, we turn outward to a belief system, some specially anointed or enlightened guru, and a set of stone tablets telling us what to do. This is exactly what the Christian religion did with Jesus. We can't help ourselves. There's something about this arrangement that makes us feel safe, secure, and superior. Maybe it's because it's the way we have been taught from birth, but it is the wrong foundation and must be abandoned. There is no salvation there.

As it stands now, we have millions of these scenarios operating. Belief systems and ideologies, ruled over by their various gurus, are being created daily, each of them promising their particular version of salvation or heaven. There are our conventional religious/spiritual belief systems pushing their slant on things, many with the threat of dire eternal consequences if we do it wrong. Some promote wonderful eternal bliss up there in the sky. Then we have those philosophies that promise abundant living on earth by applying the secret of attracting everything we want in life from a universe that is more than willing to hand it over if we want it enough. Then there are political systems that offer us the earth if we vote for them. Just when has that stuff ever worked?

One thing is for sure, we can't agree on which one is right. Many of them are complete opposites and war against each other. But despite all this variation, they all have the same common source, the human psyche. We make them up. As enticing as they may be, they are devoid of truth because they originate from those corrupt mindsets of the worldly and religious reasoning that rule within us. They are all variations of the same false logic and reasoning and come from the wrong source. Whatever we generate from the source of the human psyche—religion, spirituality, government, philosophy, altruism, entertainment—it won't work. How do we know this? Because this is what we've been doing for thousands of years and it hasn't added up to much. Yep, there go those wheels on the bus again!

Meanwhile, all the geniuses and gurus have their books, podcasts, websites, blogs, Facebook groups, and social media followers and fans, pumping out their ideas, beliefs, and teachings. The leader is carefully edited and only presents what perpetuates a persona of spirituality and enlightenment.

So it turns out that we are not very unique or creative after all. This is the exact situation Jesus confronted with the religious and worldly gurus of his day. Jesus exposed it all for the sham that it was and said that the whole mess was going to crumble to the ground. It was a pretty strong accusation for Jesus to make, and yet when Pilate had his time with Jesus, he concluded that Jesus was being led by a power, reality, and authority in which he could find no fault.

All these gurus and belief systems are competing for our attention, claiming to have the answers when we are already carrying around within us the complete answer for all eternity. How dumb can we be?!

So, we need to stick together. We can't let this happen anymore. We must avoid all temptation to turn what is real and true within us into another religion or belief system with gurus and programs. We need to help each other connect with that life-giving Spirit and source that runs through us all. When we do, we won't need all those supporting structures we have designed. This is way bigger that all that stuff. We can live in an atmosphere of love, peace, oneness, and power . . . forever.

Wow, chapter 20 is finally finished . . . or so I thought.

Come to think of it, I have books, blogs, Facebook pages, and a guru status. Damn, I have to actually apply this stuff to myself.

While those things have had a purpose, I can see they have just about reached their use-by date. This is much bigger and self-sustaining than anything I could ever come up with. It's been hard work looking after that stuff anyway. I think instead I'm just going to plug into that source right alongside you and all of us. No gurus, just all of us together as one family, helping each other and birthing the true messiah into this world so we can all share in this new reality together. We'll let that Chief Shepherd of the ages within us sort out the mess. I'm for following that higher spiritual presence.

If we listen, trust, follow. and speak from that heavenly dimension within us—which is the same nature of Jesus—we will experience ourselves as that family or household that brings the living bread into our world that triumphs, overcomes, and makes all things whole. Phew! That is just so much easier!

Jesus said, "And I, when I am lifted up from the earth, will draw all people to myself" (John 12:32). In other words, when we lift up that eternal Spirit out of ourselves, it becomes recognizable to all of humankind because it runs through each and every one of us. That power source suddenly begins to flicker as each person turns to that source within. Its power and energy will strengthen until the Spirit is aflame in all of us, and then our world will be transformed into a reality unlike any other, and it will be "on earth as it is in heaven." Every tear will be wiped away and we will live in peace, abundance, wholeness, security, well-being, and joy . . . without death . . . all of us . . . past and present . . . together . . . forever.

John Lennon and his song "Imagine" was condemned viciously by the fundamental Bible-thumping Christians as being demonic. They believed the song, and many others like it, originated from the depths of hell, and they preached against people listening to them.

Let's take a quick look at the lyrics at John Lennon's "Imagine":

Imagine there's no heaven
It's easy if you try
No hell below us
Above us only sky
Imagine all the people
Living for today . . .

Imagine there's no countries
It isn't hard to do

Nothing to kill or die for
And no religion too
Imagine all the people
Living life in peace . . .

Imagine no possessions
I wonder if you can
No need for greed or hunger
A brotherhood of man
Imagine all the people
Sharing all the world . . .

You may say I'm a dreamer
But I'm not the only one
I hope someday you'll join us
And the world will be as one . . .

Which viewpoint was demonic: John Lennon's song or the mindset and ideology that sought to squash it? Just ask inside yourself. Go deep; you will feel it bubble up. It wasn't the words John Lennon wrote, was it?

Well, I'm off to follow that higher spiritual presence that's within me and each of us. You might say I'm a dreamer. But I'm not the only one.

Are you coming too?

ABOUT THE AUTHOR

JIM PALMER IS AN ORDAINED MINISTER, AUTHOR, ACTIVIST, SPEAKER, SPIRITUAL DIRECTOR, AND LEADING FIGURE IN THE NON-RELIGIOUS SPIRITUALITY MOVEMENT.

Palmer received his master of divinity degree from Trinity Divinity School in Chicago and served several years as a Christian pastor. In 2000, Palmer left professional ministry and began chronicling his journey of "shedding religion to find God."

After leaving professional Christian ministry, Palmer served as U.S. Director of Education for International Justice Mission (IJM), an international human rights organization in Washington, D.C. He traveled through South Asia with IJM as part of an operation to free children from forced child prostitution and child slave labor. He is currently an adjunct college professor of Ethics, Linguistics, and Comparative Religions in Nashville. In 2012, Palmer founded The Religion-Free Bible Project, an effort to create a paraphrase of the Bible, free from the religious bias that Palmer believes has been imposed on it.

Palmer actively promotes causes that have touched his life. Diagnosed as a child with Tourette's syndrome (TS), he raises awareness about the disorder and corresponds extensively with others who suffer from TS and parents of children with TS. As a result of Palmer's work with International Justice Mission, he consistently speaks out about human rights issues, including forced child prostitution and child slave labor. He currently lives with his family in Nashville, Tennessee.

Jim's personal interests include cycling, abstract art, animals, music, and hanging out with family and friends. He connects with people through social media on Facebook, Twitter, and jimpalmerblog.com.

More books by Jim Palmer:

Divine Nobodies:
Shedding Religion to Find God
(and the unlikely people who help you)

Wide Open Spaces:
Beyond Paint-by-Number Christianity

Being Jesus in Nashville:
Finding the Courage to Live Your Life
(Whoever and Wherever You Are)

Notes from (Over) the Edge:
Unmasking the Truth to End Your Suffering

Printed in Great Britain
by Amazon

83626368R00098